F*CK PERFECT

F*CK PERFECT

DERRICK C SOLANO

CONTENTS

To the ones who've been told they're not enough—this is for you.

To those who've fought battles no one else can see, carried scars the world tried to shame, and kept standing even when everything around you fell apart. This book is your reminder that you're not just enough—you're everything.

To Caleb, my son, my heart, my silent prayer every day. Even though life pulled us apart, my love for you has never wavered. Every page I've written is infused with the hope that wherever you are, you're thriving, happy, and loved. You are always with me.

To Anthony, my rock, my peace, and the reason I know what unconditional love feels like. You've stood by me through the chaos, the growth, and the rebirth, reminding me every day that the quiet moments we share are life's greatest gift. You are my anchor, my safe place, my always.

To Blanca, Jacki, Pebbles, Billie, Raina, Charlie, Chelsea, Chandler, and every other furry companion who's shared my journey. Your unconditional loyalty and love have taught me what it means to live in the moment and find joy even in the simplest things.

To my readers—you brave, messy, beautiful souls. Thank you for letting my story be part of yours. This book is for every person who's felt broken, abandoned, or lost and decided to rise anyway. You are the reason I wrote this. You are my inspiration, my fuel, and my proof that no one has to go through this life alone.

And finally, to the person I used to be—the scared, lost, angry kid who thought he'd never be enough. You made it. Your scars became your strength, and you learned to turn pain into power. This book is my goodbye to you, but also my eternal thank you. Without you, I

Part One: Burn the Bullsh*t

Alright, let's kick this off the only way that makes sense: by lighting a fire under all the crap that's been holding you back. Society loves to shove this idea of perfection down our throats, like we're all supposed to wake up with Instagram-ready lives, a six-figure job, perfect abs, and a deep love for kale smoothies. Let me be clear: that's not life. That's bullsh*t wrapped in a filter. And if you're reading this, I'm guessing you've had enough of it, too.

This part of the book is where we rip off the Band-Aid and start dismantling the lies we've been sold since birth. You know the ones: "Be good," "Don't make waves," "Stay in your lane," "Work hard and everything will magically fall into place." Spoiler alert—none of that sh*t works. Life doesn't play by those rules, and honestly, it's exhausting trying to keep up with expectations that were never meant for real, flawed, messy human beings like us.

I've spent years trying to be what everyone else wanted me to be—a perfect son, a perfect partner, a perfect psychic, even. You name it, I've tried it. And you know what all that effort got me? A one-way ticket to rock bottom with a side of shame and self-loathing. I spent so much time twisting myself into someone else's version of "good enough" that I lost sight of who the hell I actually was. And if you've been there—if you've ever felt like you're suffocating under the weight of everyone else's opinions—then welcome. You're in the right place.

In this first part, we're going to burn it all down. The myths. The expectations. The idea that you have to play by someone else's rules to matter. We're going to take a hard, unfiltered look at the stories you've been telling yourself—stories you probably didn't even write. I'm going to share the moments in my life where I finally said, "F*ck this," and stopped trying to live up to someone else's version of who I should be. From the foster care system to broken relationships to crawling out of a jail cell with nothing but scars and determination, I learned the hard way that perfection isn't just unattainable—it's a lie. A destructive, soul-sucking lie.

So, consider this your permission slip to stop giving a damn about what anyone else thinks. Whether it's your family, your boss, your neighbors, or that random person on Facebook who wouldn't know real life if it smacked them in the face, their opinions don't mean sh*t. The only thing that matters is what you want, what you value, and how you choose to show up in this world—scars, mistakes, and all.

This part isn't going to be gentle. It's not about making you feel good or patting you on the back while you quietly stay stuck in the same old patterns. Nope. We're here to throw some gasoline on those tired old excuses and watch them go up in flames. And yeah, I'll throw in some humor, because if we can't laugh at how absurd life is, what's the point? But make no mistake—this is where the real work begins.

Are you ready to burn the bullsh*t? Good. Let's light the match.

CHAPTER ONE

The Perfect Lie

Perfection. The shiny, unattainable carrot dangled in front of every one of us since birth. It's like that kid in school who always had the newest gadgets, perfect hair, and a lunchbox full of snacks you'd kill for—except now, instead of a kid, it's a whole damn society telling you to keep chasing this illusion of flawlessness. The perfect job, the perfect body, the perfect family, the perfect life. And let me tell you something right out of the gate: it's all a steaming pile of bullsh*t.

The idea of perfection is the biggest con ever pulled. It's like the timeshare of life goals—sounds good at first, but once you buy in, you're trapped paying for something you'll never actually use. Perfection is designed to keep you running in circles, jumping through hoops for approval that doesn't matter from people you don't even like. It's a scam, plain and simple, and if you're reading this thinking, "Yeah, but I've just about got it all figured out," let me save you the suspense. You don't. Nobody does. And anyone who says otherwise is either lying or has a stick so far up their ass it's basically a spinal column.

Here's the truth: perfection doesn't exist. At least not in the way they sell it to us. You're never going to be flawless, mistake-free, or universally loved. You're never going to have it all together 24/7. Hell, you're not supposed to. Life is messy, and the sooner you stop trying to clean it up for Instagram, the better off you'll be. I spent years of my life trying to live up to this idea of what I thought people wanted me to be. I tried to be the perfect son, the perfect partner, the perfect person who never got angry, never made waves, never f*cked up. *You know what it got me? A one-way ticket to a jail cell, a shattered sense of self, and a front-row seat to my own bullsh*t.

But let's back up for a second and talk about where this whole "perfect" scam comes from. Spoiler alert: it starts early. Remember being a kid and getting told to "be good," "behave," "sit still," or "act right"? Yeah, same. They start programming us before we even know what's happening, drilling into our heads that if we just try hard enough, we'll get the gold star. And maybe you did get a few gold stars along the way—straight A's, a promotion, an "I'm so proud of you" from someone you wanted to impress. But was it ever enough? Did it ever make you feel complete? Or did it just make you want more stars?

That's the lie. The myth of perfection isn't about helping you grow or thrive—it's about keeping you on the hamster wheel. They want you to keep striving, keep buying, keep chasing something you'll never catch because if you ever stopped and realized you were already good enough, their whole system would fall apart. The truth is, "perfect" isn't about you at all. It's about control. It's about making sure you stay busy doubting yourself instead of questioning why you're being fed this bullsh*t in the first place.

Let me give you a real-life example of what chasing perfection looks like. Back in the day, when I was trying to build a life with Hope—my first serious relationship—I wanted so badly to be the perfect boyfriend, the perfect man, the perfect provider. I bent over backwards to make sure she had everything she wanted, even if it meant burying my own needs so deep they were practically fossils. I even committed identity theft to get furniture, thinking, "If our place looks perfect, maybe we'll be happy." Spoiler alert: we weren't. Not even close. Turns out, you can't buy your way to happiness, and you sure as hell can't fake your way to it, either. That little stunt landed me in jail, stripped of everything I thought made me "enough." And you know what? That was the best thing that ever happened to me. Because once I lost everything, I realized I didn't need to be perfect. I just needed to be real.

The problem with perfection is that it's all about appearances. It's about what other people think, not about what actually matters to you. And let me tell you, living for other people's approval is the fastest way to lose yourself. You start making choices based on what you think will impress others, not on what actually feels right for you. You sacrifice your authenticity on the altar of "good enough," and the worst part is, nobody even cares. All those people you're bending over backwards to please? They're too busy worrying about their own sh*t to notice. So why the hell are you giving their opinions so much power?

Here's the kicker: the things that make you "imperfect" are the things that make you human. Your flaws, your quirks, your mistakes—they're not weaknesses. They're your f*cking superpowers. They're what make you unique, what give you depth, what make you relatable. Trying to hide them in pursuit of perfection is like throwing away your favorite jeans because they've got a rip in them. That rip is what makes them badass. It tells a story. And guess what? So do you.

So, let's stop the madness. Let's stop chasing this impossible standard that only serves to make us miserable. Let's call perfection what it really is: a lie. A shiny, toxic, soul-sucking lie. And instead of wasting our time trying to be something we're not, let's focus on being exactly who we are—messy, flawed, and beautifully human. Because that? That's where the magic happens. That's where life gets real. And if you ask me, that's the only kind of perfect worth striving for.

CHAPTER TWO

F*ck Their Opinions

Here's the deal: everyone has an opinion about your life, and 99.9% of them are total garbage. Some people hand them out like business cards—unsolicited, unnecessary, and always at the worst possible time. "You should try this," "Why don't you do that?" "Oh, I could *never* live like you." You know what? F*ck their opinions. Unless someone is paying your bills, walking in your shoes, or wiping your ass, their opinion about your life is worth less than the gum stuck to the bottom of your shoe.

Let's get one thing straight: most people's opinions have nothing to do with you and everything to do with them. They're projecting their own insecurities, fears, and frustrations onto you because it's easier than dealing with their own sh*t. *They see you trying something new, chasing your dreams, or just living your truth, and it makes them uncomfortable. Why? Because your freedom reminds them of their chains. Your courage makes them aware of their cowardice. Your "I don't give a fck" attitude* shines a light on their desperate need for approval. And instead of clapping for you, they try to drag you down to their level. Misery loves company, after all.

Let me tell you a story to prove my point. Back when I first started doing psychic readings, I got a lot of side-eye. People had opinions for days. Some thought it was a scam. Others thought it was "weird" or "fake." Hell, even people I thought had my back would make snide little comments like, "So… you talk to ghosts now?" Yeah, Karen, and they told me you should worry less about me and more about your sh*tty marriage. But I didn't say that. I smiled, I nodded, and then I kept doing my thing because I knew their judgment wasn't about me. It was about them. I was stepping into something they didn't understand, and instead of being curious or supportive, they defaulted to criticism.

Here's the punchline: those same people who doubted me, talked sh*t, and rolled their eyes? They were the first ones in line when my readings took off. Suddenly, I wasn't "weird" anymore—I was "amazing," "talented," "gifted." Funny how that works, right? The truth is, people will criticize you right up until you prove them wrong. And even then, they'll find a way to make it about themselves.

The lesson? Don't let other people's opinions dictate your decisions. If I had listened to all those voices telling me what I could or couldn't do, I'd still be sitting in the wreckage of my old life, too scared to take a single step forward. Instead, I learned to tune out the noise and trust myself. I leaned into what felt right for me, even when it made other people uncomfortable. And guess what? That's when my life started to change.

But let's be real—it's not easy to ignore the haters, especially when they're people you care about. It hits different when the criticism comes from your family, your friends, or your partner. You want their support. You want them to believe in you. And when they don't, it stings. I know that feeling all too well. When I was fighting to stay afloat—losing Caleb, crawling out of addiction, trying to piece together some semblance of a life—I was desperate for someone, anyone, to tell me I was on the right track. Instead, I got silence. Or worse, judgment disguised as advice. "You should focus on getting a real job." "Maybe you're just not meant to have custody." "Why don't you try being normal for once?" Yeah, thanks for that groundbreaking insight, but I think I'll pass.

Eventually, I realized something that changed everything: you don't need anyone else's permission to live your life. You don't need their approval, their understanding, or their validation. Because at the end of the day, the only person who has to live with your choices is you. They don't have to walk your path, deal with your struggles, or fight your battles. So why the f*ck should they get a say in how you live?

Here's the harsh truth: no matter what you do, someone's going to have a problem with it. If you play it safe, they'll call you boring. If you take risks, they'll say you're reckless. If you succeed, they'll call you lucky. If you fail, they'll call you foolish. You can't win. So stop trying. Instead of chasing approval, focus on chasing what feels right for you. Build a life that makes you happy, not one that makes other people comfortable.

Does that mean you should ignore all advice? Not necessarily. If someone you trust offers constructive feedback that comes from a place of love, listen. But there's a big difference between helpful advice and toxic opinions. Helpful advice respects your autonomy. It offers insight without demanding obedience. Toxic opinions, on the other hand, are all about control. They're designed to keep you small, scared, and dependent on someone else's validation. Learn to tell the difference, and don't be afraid to set boundaries with people who can't respect your choices.

At the end of the day, your life is yours. Not your mom's, not your boss's, not your nosy neighbor's—yours. So *fck their opinions. Wear the outfit, start the business, take the trip, follow the dream. Do the thing that sets your soul on fire, even if it pisses some people off. Because those who truly love you will cheer you on, no matter how unconventional your path may be. And the rest? Well, they can fck all the way off.*

CHAPTER THREE

You're Not That Special (And That's Okay)

Let me hit you with some truth right out of the gate: you're not that special. Don't freak out yet—hear me out. You're not some unicorn with a destiny to cure cancer, end world hunger, and be universally adored by everyone you meet. You're a regular-ass human like the rest of us, stumbling through life with a mix of wins, losses, and a whole lot of messy in between. And guess what? That's f*cking beautiful.

We live in a world that's obsessed with being "special." Social media has turned every moment into a highlight reel, and now everyone feels like they have to be extraordinary just to be worth a second glance. It's exhausting. If you're not climbing Everest while starting a billion-dollar company and rescuing puppies on the side, it's easy to feel like you're falling short. But let me tell you something life-changing: being ordinary is underrated. Real happiness isn't about being special—it's about being real.

You don't have to save the world to matter. You don't have to prove your worth to anyone, least of all to a society that values likes and followers over authenticity. If you're out here thinking, "But I want to make a difference!"—good. That's great. But here's the kicker: you don't have to change the whole world to change *someone's* world. Sometimes, the most impactful thing you can do is just show up as your honest, flawed, incredible self.

Now, I know this might sting a little. We all grew up hearing that we were "special," right? Our parents told us we were destined for greatness, that we could be anything we wanted, that we were the main character in the story of life. And while that's a lovely sentiment, it's also bullsh*t if you take it too literally. Life doesn't give a damn about your main-character energy. It's not a movie where you're guaranteed a happy ending just because you've got good intentions and a quirky personality. Life is messy, random, and unfair. But it's also breathtakingly beautiful in ways that have nothing to do with being special.

Let me break it down for you: being "not special" doesn't mean you're not important. It doesn't mean your life lacks value. It just means you don't have to carry the weight of the world on your shoulders. You don't have to be the best, the brightest, or the most anything to live a life that matters. And once you let go of the pressure to be extraordinary, you can finally start enjoying the f*cking ride.

Here's a story for you. Back in my early 20s, I thought I had to prove myself to everyone. After all the sh*t I'd been through—the foster homes, the betrayals, losing Caleb—I was desperate to show the world that I could rise above it all and become someone worth noticing. I threw myself into work, relationships, and anything else that seemed like it might validate me. I wanted to be admired. Respected. Loved. But you know what? None of it worked. No matter how hard I tried to be "special," I always felt like I was falling short. And the harder I tried, the more miserable I became.

It wasn't until I hit rock bottom—sitting in that Texas jail cell, stripped of everything I thought made me valuable—that I realized I'd been chasing the wrong goal. I didn't need to be extraordinary. I didn't need to impress anyone. I just needed to figure out who the hell I was and start living for myself. That moment, as painful and humiliating as it was, set me free. I stopped trying to be special and started trying to be *real*. And you know what? That's when sh*t started to change.

When you stop trying to be special, you give yourself permission to just *be*. You stop comparing your life to everyone else's highlight reel. You stop measuring your worth by achievements, titles, or applause. And you start appreciating the little things—the moments that make life worth living, even if they don't come with a trophy or a viral post.

Look, it's okay to have big dreams. It's okay to want to make an impact. But don't let the pursuit of "special" steal the joy from your ordinary moments. The truth is, some of the most meaningful parts of life are the ones that happen quietly, away from the spotlight. Like sitting on the couch with someone you love, laughing until your stomach hurts. Or taking your dog for a walk and watching them lose their sh*t over a stick. Or even just getting through a tough day and knowing you didn't give up.

Life isn't about being extraordinary—it's about finding the magic in the ordinary. And the best part? Once you stop trying to be special, you start to realize just how amazing you already are. Not because you've achieved something grand, but because you're here. Alive. Breathing. Doing your best, even when it's hard. That's enough. You're enough.

So, let's make a deal. Stop trying to be "special," and start focusing on what actually matters. Show up for yourself. Show up for the people you love. Do things that make your soul happy, even if they're not Instagram-worthy. Because at the end of the day, being real is way better than being special. And if you ask me, it's a hell of a lot more fun, too.

Sh*t Happens

Here's the thing about life: it doesn't give a single *fck about your plans. You can map out your future, color-code your calendar, and vision-board the hell out of your dreams, but life? Life will still throw a curveball, flip the table, and set the whole thing on fire just because it can. And honestly? That's okay. Because the sooner you accept that sh*t happens,* the sooner you can stop wasting energy on what you can't control and start focusing on what you can.

Let me say this loud and clear: sh*t doesn't happen *to* you; it just happens. Life isn't out to get you, and there's no universal conspiracy to ruin your day. It just *is*. Sometimes the universe decides you need a flat tire, or your boss needs to be an asshole, or your cat needs to puke on your favorite hoodie. It sucks, it's inconvenient, and it can throw your whole vibe off, but it's not personal. The world isn't plotting against you—it's just doing what it does.

Take it from me, I've seen sh*t hit the fan in every way imaginable. From being abandoned as a kid to losing Caleb to finding myself in a jail cell wondering how the hell I got there, I've been through some seriously messed-up situations. And let me tell you, spending all your time asking, "Why me?" doesn't change a damn thing. The real question isn't "Why did this happen?" but "What the fck am I going to do about it?"*

Let me take you back to one of my favorite examples of life flipping me the bird. Picture this: I'm 22 years old, sitting in an ICU bed after trying to check out of life for good. My body is wrecked, my spirit is shattered, and my mind is stuck in this endless loop of regret and hopelessness. I had nothing left—no family, no freedom, no future. If you'd told me in that moment that one day I'd be writing books, sharing my story, and helping other people rise from their own ashes, I would've laughed in your face. Or maybe cried. Probably both.

But you know what? That rock-bottom moment was the wake-up call I needed. It was the universe's way of saying, "You've got two choices: stay down or get the f*ck up." And while it wasn't easy, I eventually chose the latter. I didn't get there overnight, and it wasn't pretty, but I made it. Not because life suddenly got better or easier, but because I stopped expecting it to. I stopped waiting for the universe to cut me a break and started figuring out how to work with what I had.

Here's the truth: bad things are going to happen. People will hurt you, plans will fall apart, and sometimes it'll feel like the universe is trying to break you. But here's the secret: you can't break what refuses to stay broken. The moment you stop resisting life's chaos and start adapting to it, you become unbreakable. You turn every piece of sh*t *life throws at you into fertilizer for your growth. Yeah, I know that sounds cheesy, but it's also true. Sh*t* happens, but you get to decide what you do with it.

Now, let's talk about control, or the lack of it. Most of the stress we feel when sh*t *goes wrong comes from this illusion that we're supposed to be in control of everything. Spoiler alert: you're not. And that's a good thing. Because if you were in control of everything, you'd probably f*ck it up* anyway. Life is unpredictable, and that's what makes it interesting. You can't stop the storms from coming, but you can learn how to dance in the rain. Or at least not drown in it.

So, how do you deal with sh*t *when it happens? Step one: take a deep breath and accept it. I know that sounds simple, but trust me, it's powerful. The more you fight reality, the more miserable you'll be. Step two: figure out what you can control. Maybe you can't fix the situation, but you can control how you react to it. Step three: laugh at it. Seriously, humor is one of the best tools you have. When life hands you a sh*t* sandwich, sometimes the only thing you can do is laugh at the absurdity of it all.

Take my jail experience, for example. When I was sitting in that cold Texas cell waiting to be transferred back to Arizona, I could've spent all my time stewing in anger and self-pity. And yeah, I did that for a bit. But eventually, I started finding the humor in the situation. Like the fact that my cellmate snored louder than a chainsaw, or that I actually missed the crappy furniture I stole with someone else's credit. Laughing didn't change my circumstances, but it made them a hell of a lot easier to bear.

And that's the point: you can't stop sh*t from happening, but you can decide how you're going to handle it. You can let it crush you, or you can let it shape you. You can wallow in the unfairness of it all, or you can stand up, brush yourself off, and say, "Is that all you've got?"

Life is messy, unpredictable, and often downright infuriating. But it's also beautiful, hilarious, and full of surprises. So, the next time sh*t *hits the fan, remember this: it's not the end of the world. It's just life being life. And you? You're tougher than you think. You've got this. Now go out there and turn that sh*t* into something amazing. Or at least something you can laugh about later.

CHAPTER FIVE

The World Doesn't Give a F*ck (So You Should)

Let me start by letting you in on a little secret: the world doesn't give a f*ck about you. Not in the "nobody loves you" sense—don't spiral, calm down. I mean that the universe isn't sitting around, plotting your success or failure. It's not tailoring its storms to ruin your day or sprinkling fairy dust to make your dreams come true. The world is indifferent. And weirdly, that's the best news you'll hear all day.

Here's why: when you realize the world doesn't care, you're free. Free from the pressure to perform, to prove yourself, or to live up to some imaginary standard that doesn't exist. You're free to stop waiting for the stars to align and start aligning your own damn self. Because if the world doesn't give a f*ck, then the only person who really needs to care about your life is you.

This isn't some nihilistic "nothing matters" rant. Quite the opposite, actually. It's a call to action. If you want something, you have to go after it. If you care about something, you have to protect it. If you value your time, energy, and sanity, you have to guard them like a dragon sitting on a pile of gold. Because no one else is going to do it for you. The world won't hand you sh*t, but it also won't stop you from going out and taking what you need. That's the beauty of it.

Take my life, for example. If I had waited for the world to care about me—if I'd sat around hoping someone would swoop in and save me—I'd still be rotting in that Texas jail cell, drowning in self-pity and broken dreams. Nobody was going to write me a redemption arc. Nobody was going to hand me a clean slate and say, "Here you go, Derrick, take a second chance." The world didn't care if I stayed down. So, I had to care enough to get back up.

And that's the thing: when you care about yourself—really, truly give a sh*t about your life—you stop waiting for permission to live it. You stop looking for validation from people who don't matter. You stop blaming the universe for your problems and start taking responsibility for your choices. And yeah, it's scary as hell. But it's also the most empowering thing you'll ever do.

Now, let's talk about why people get stuck. A lot of folks are waiting for someone or something to give them a green light. They think they need the world's approval to chase their dreams, speak their truth, or even just exist. Guess what? You don't. The world doesn't give a *fck if you start that business, write that book, or finally tell your boss to shove it. So why the hell are you waiting for its blessing? Spoiler alert: it's not coming. And that's a good thing. Because if nobody's watching, you can do whatever the f*ck you want.*

This isn't about recklessness—it's about freedom. When you stop caring about what the world thinks, you start focusing on what you think. You start asking yourself questions like, "What do I actually want?" and "What matters to me?" And when you find those answers, you go after them like your life depends on it. Because, spoiler alert, it does.

I'll give you a real-life example. When I started writing **I Won't Break**, I wasn't thinking about whether the world would care. I wasn't writing for the New York Times or Oprah's Book Club. I was writing for me—and for the people who needed to hear my story. I didn't care if it sold a million copies or just one, as long as that one person felt less alone. And you know what? That mindset made all the difference. Because when you stop worrying about who's watching, you can finally start creating something real.

But let me warn you: this isn't an excuse to stop caring altogether. The world doesn't give a f*ck, but that doesn't mean you shouldn't. Caring is your superpower. It's what drives you to fight for what you believe in, to stand up for yourself, and to chase the life you want. The trick is knowing where to direct that care. Don't waste it on things you can't control, people who don't value it, or goals that don't align with your truth. Save it for the things that set your soul on fire.

At the end of the day, the world's indifference is your opportunity. It's your chance to stop living for other people's expectations and start living for yourself. So, take the risk. Make the move. Do the thing you've been too scared to try. Because the world isn't going to stop you—and that's all the permission you'll ever need.

Part Two: Unmasking Your Truth

Alright, now that we've torched the bullsh*t, *it's time to get real—like, uncomfortably real. This part of the book is where we stop pretending, peel back the layers, and figure out who the f*ck you actually* are underneath all the masks you've been wearing. You know the ones: the "I've got my sh*t together" mask, the "I'm fine, really" mask, the "please like me" mask. Yeah, those. They've gotta go.

Here's the thing about masks: they might feel like armor, but they're actually just cages. Sure, they protect you from judgment and rejection, but they also keep you from connection, authenticity, and freedom. They trap you in a version of yourself that isn't real, and worse, they trick you into believing that the real you isn't good enough. Newsflash: it is. You are. And the sooner you let go of the masks, the sooner you can start living the life you've been pretending to have all along.

Unmasking your truth isn't easy. It's raw, messy, and sometimes downright scary. But it's also liberating as f*ck. When you stop hiding behind what you think people want to see, you make room for who you really are—flaws, scars, and all. And trust me, the world needs the real you, not the polished, filtered, watered-down version you've been showing off. The real you is where the magic happens.

In this part of the book, we're going to dive into the art of unmasking. We'll talk about owning your sh*t, *embracing your flaws, and learning to love yourself without all the filters. We'll dig into why you started wearing masks in the first place (hint: it's not your fault), and how to let go of them without losing your damn mind. And yeah, we'll do it with a* *healthy dose of humor, because if we can't laugh at ourselves while we're getting our sh*t together, what's the point?*

This isn't about becoming a "better" version of yourself—it's about becoming the *realest* version of yourself. It's about showing up in the world as the messy, glorious, imperfect human you are and saying, "This is me. Take it or leave it." So, are you ready to unmask your truth? Let's do this.

CHAPTER SIX

Take Off the Mask

Let's talk about masks. Not the fun ones you wear on Halloween or the face masks that make you look like a swamp monster while promising to clear your pores. I'm talking about the masks we wear every single day—the ones that say, "Everything's fine," when it's really not. The ones that smile when you want to scream. The ones that fit so perfectly, even you forget they're there.

We all wear masks. Hell, some of us have an entire collection. There's the "I've got my sh*t together" mask, the "perfect parent" mask, the "I'm tough, I don't need anyone" mask. And let's not forget the crowd favorite: the "everything's fine" mask. We slap these things on to protect ourselves, to fit in, to avoid judgment or rejection. And yeah, they might do the job for a while. But here's the problem: masks don't just hide your flaws—they hide your truth. They suffocate the real you.

For most of my life, I was a master mask-wearer. Growing up in the foster care system, I learned early on that showing vulnerability was like painting a target on my back. So, I became whoever I thought people wanted me to be. The "good kid," the "strong one," the "kid who didn't need help." Later, I added new masks to the collection: the "perfect boyfriend," the "successful psychic," the "man who had it all figured out." And let me tell you, I played those roles so well, I started believing them myself. But deep down, I knew it was all bullsh*t. The real me was buried under so many layers, I didn't even know who I was anymore.

The truth hit me like a freight train the day I landed in that Texas jail cell. There were no masks in there. No roles to play, no persona to uphold, no one left to impress. It was just me—raw, broken, and exposed. And you know what? That moment, as humiliating as it was, saved me. Because when you're stripped down to nothing, you finally get a chance to figure out who the f*ck you really are.

So, let me ask you: who are you without the masks? If you weren't trying to impress anyone or live up to anyone's expectations, what would you look like? What would you sound like? What would you want? It's a terrifying question, I know. Because taking off the mask means risking rejection. It means risking failure. It means standing in front of the world and saying, "This is me," knowing full well that not everyone will like what they see. But here's the thing: not everyone has to. The people who matter—the ones who truly see you, love you, and accept you—can't do that if you're hiding behind a mask.

I get it, though. Taking off the mask is scary as hell. It's easier to keep playing the role, to keep pretending, to keep telling yourself that maybe, just maybe, the mask is who you really are. But let me tell you something I've learned the hard way: masks don't protect you; they isolate you. They keep you from forming real connections, real love, and real happiness. Because how can anyone love the real you if you're too scared to show them?

Now, I'm not saying you need to rip off the mask and start screaming your deepest secrets to strangers in the grocery store. This isn't about oversharing—it's about authenticity. It's about getting real with yourself first, so you can start showing up as the person you were meant to be. And that starts with asking yourself some hard questions: What am

I hiding? Who am I trying to impress? What would happen if I stopped pretending?

When I finally started peeling back my masks, it wasn't pretty. There were a lot of tears, a lot of anger, and a whole lot of "What the f*ck am I doing?" But with every layer I shed, I felt lighter. Freer. Stronger. And yeah, not everyone liked the real me. Some people bailed. Some people didn't understand. But the ones who stayed? Those are my people. Those are the ones who saw me for who I was and loved me anyway.

Here's the thing: you don't owe anyone perfection. You don't owe them the polished, filtered, socially acceptable version of yourself. What you owe—to yourself and the people who truly matter—is honesty. And honesty doesn't mean being perfect; it means being real. So, take off the mask. Let the world see your scars, your quirks, your beautifully messy truth. Because that's where the magic is. That's where life gets real. And trust me, it's worth it.

CHAPTER SEVEN

Own the Ugly

Let's get one thing straight right now: we've all got some ugly. I'm not just talking about the bad selfies, the questionable fashion choices, or the time you drunkenly sang karaoke and ended up on someone's Instagram. No, I'm talking about the stuff you try to bury deep down—the mistakes, the bad habits, the cringe-worthy sh*t you've done, and the parts of yourself you wish you could Photoshop out of existence. Guess what? That's your ugly. And it's time to own it.

Owning your ugly isn't about loving every little flaw and pretending you're totally fine with all your baggage. That's bullsh*t. *No one wakes up thinking, "Man, I really love how I f*cked up that relationship back in 2017."* What it's really about is facing the parts of yourself that make you wince and saying, "Yeah, that's me. And I'm still standing."

For most of my life, I did everything I could to hide my ugly. I wanted so badly to look like I had it all together—a perfect facade to cover up the cracks. But no matter how hard I tried, the ugly always found a way to creep through. Like when I got caught stealing credit to buy furniture because I thought it would fix my failing relationship. Or when I pushed people away because I didn't think I deserved their love. Or the countless times I made choices I wasn't proud of, just to escape the pain I didn't know how to deal with.

For years, I carried shame like it was a full-time job. I thought that if people saw the real me—the messy, flawed, sometimes downright ugly me—they'd walk away. So, I buried it. I slapped on a smile, pretended I was fine, and hoped no one would notice the chaos lurking just beneath the surface. Spoiler alert: they noticed. Because here's the truth: no matter how much you try to hide your ugly, it always shows up eventually. And the more you deny it, the more power it has over you.

The turning point for me came when I was sitting in that ICU bed after trying to check out of life completely. I'd hit rock bottom in every possible way, and there was no hiding it anymore. My ugly was out there for the world to see. And you know what? It was freeing as hell. Because once you've been stripped of everything—your dignity, your masks, your bullsh*t—you realize that the only way out is through. You can't run from your ugly. You have to own it.

So, what does owning your ugly actually look like? First, it's about taking an honest inventory of your sh*t. Not in a "let's wallow in self-pity" kind of way, but in a "let's face this so it doesn't own me" kind of way. Look at the things you've been avoiding—your regrets, your mistakes, your insecurities—and call them out. Name them. Write them down if you have to. Because the more you acknowledge them, the less power they have over you.

Second, you've got to forgive yourself. This is the hard part, I know. We're so good at beating ourselves up for all the ways we think we've fallen short. But let me tell you something: holding onto shame doesn't make you a better person. It just keeps you stuck. Forgiveness doesn't mean excusing the sh*tty things you've done; it means giving yourself permission to move forward. It means saying, "Yeah, I f*cked up, but I'm still worthy of love, happiness, and a fresh start."

Third, you've got to own your ugly out loud. I'm not saying you need to broadcast your darkest secrets to the world (unless you're writing a book, in which case, go for it). But you do need to stop hiding it from the people who matter. When you show up as your whole, unpolished self, you give others permission to do the same. And that's where real connection happens—not in the curated, filtered moments, but in the raw, messy truth.

Let me give you an example. When I first started opening up about my past—my struggles with addiction, my time in foster care, my mistakes as a father—I was terrified. I thought people would judge me, reject me, maybe even hate me for the choices I'd made. But the opposite happened. The more I owned my ugly, the more people related to me. They didn't see me as some f*ck-up—they saw me as human. And that's the thing: your ugly isn't what makes you unlovable. It's what makes you relatable.

So, stop running from your ugly. Stop trying to scrub it away or hide it behind a shiny facade. Instead, look it in the eye and say, "Yeah, I've got some sh*t. Who doesn't?" Because here's the truth: your ugly is part of your story, and your story matters. Every mistake, every misstep, every scar—it's all part of what makes you who you are. And who you are is enough.

Owning your ugly isn't easy. It takes courage, honesty, and a whole lot of self-compassion. But it's also the most liberating thing you'll ever do. Because when you stop hiding, you start living. And when you start living, you realize that your ugly isn't something to be ashamed of—it's something to be proud of. It's proof that you've survived, that you've grown, and that you're still here, fighting for the life you deserve. And if that's not beautiful, I don't know what is.

CHAPTER EIGHT

Mirror, Mirror, F*ck You Too

L et's have a real talk about mirrors—the literal ones hanging on your wall and the figurative ones you avoid in your head. Both can be a pain in the ass. Standing in front of a mirror can feel like staring at a funhouse distortion of yourself. Every wrinkle, blemish, scar, or stretch mark seems magnified. And that's just the physical side of things. The real mirror—the one that reflects who you are, not just how you look—is a whole other level of brutal. It forces you to see yourself, flaws and all, and let's be honest: that sh*t isn't always pretty.

Mirrors are honest, though, and that's what makes them terrifying. They don't give a damn about your excuses, your Instagram filters, or the version of yourself you carefully curate for the world. They just reflect what's there. And while we can argue that beauty is in the eye of the beholder, when the beholder is you, it's often the eye of your harshest critic.

I've had my share of mirror battles. Literal ones, sure—I spent years avoiding my reflection unless I absolutely had to—but the metaphorical ones are what really f*cked with me. The moments when I had to face who I was, what I'd done, and the choices that got me to some of the darkest points in my life. When you're staring down the barrel of your own truth, there's no makeup or clever angles to hide behind. The question is: what the hell do you do with what you see?

For a long time, I hated what I saw. I don't mean I disliked it or felt a little insecure—I mean I straight-up loathed it. The guy looking back at me was someone I didn't recognize, someone I didn't even want to know. He was the sum of every mistake I'd ever made, every time I'd let someone down, every scar I'd tried to hide. That reflection was a constant reminder of everything I thought I wasn't: good enough, strong enough, lovable enough.

Take the ICU moment I mentioned earlier in this book. After my attempt to escape life permanently, I woke up surrounded by machines, wires, and that sterile hospital smell that screams "rock bottom." But it wasn't the tubes in my arms or the pity in the nurse's eyes that broke me—it was catching my reflection in the window late one night. I looked like sh*t, sure, but what I saw in my eyes was worse: hopelessness. That reflection whispered, "You're a failure, Derrick. You're broken. You're done." And for a while, I believed it.

But here's the thing about mirrors—they don't just show you who you are; they also show you who you can become. That night in the ICU, after staring at myself for what felt like hours, something shifted. I realized I didn't have to accept the person I saw. I didn't have to let that reflection define me. If I hated what I saw, I had two choices: keep hating it or do something about it. And as much as I wanted to give up, I chose the latter. Because as brutal as mirrors can be, they're also a challenge. They dare you to own your sh*t and grow from it.

But let's get practical here. How the hell do you face the mirror when all it does is scream your flaws back at you? First, you've got to understand that your reflection isn't the enemy. It's just a snapshot—a moment in time. It doesn't define your worth or your potential. It's just a tool, a starting point. And like any tool, it can be used for good or bad. The choice is yours.

Second, stop focusing solely on the things you don't like. I get it—when you look in the mirror, your eyes immediately zero in on that zit, those extra pounds, or the dark circles under your eyes. But try shifting your focus. Find one thing—just one—that you like, or at least don't hate. Maybe it's your hair, your smile, or even the way your nose crinkles when you laugh. Start small. Build from there. Over time, you'll train yourself to see more than just the flaws.

Third, start talking back to your reflection. I know it sounds cheesy, but hear me out. The things you say to yourself in the mirror matter. If you're constantly tearing yourself down, you're reinforcing those negative beliefs. Instead, try flipping the script. Look yourself in the eye and say something kind, even if it feels fake at first. "You're doing your best." "You're stronger than you think." "You're a badass." Say it like you mean it, and eventually, you will.

Now, let's talk about the metaphorical mirror—the one that forces you to face who you are, not just how you look. This one's harder because it cuts deeper. It's not about surface-level insecurities; it's about the beliefs, fears, and regrets that shape how you see yourself. To face this mirror, you have to get brutally honest with yourself. You have to own your mistakes, forgive your flaws, and let go of the guilt that keeps you stuck.

For me, this meant confronting some hard truths. I had to own the fact that I'd made decisions that hurt people, including myself. I had to face the guilt of losing Caleb and the shame of not being the father I wanted to be. I had to stop running from my past and start owning it. And let me tell you, it was ugly, messy, and painful as hell. But it was also liberating. Because once you own your truth, no one can use it against you.

Here's the reality: you're never going to love everything about yourself. That's not the goal. The goal is to make peace with who you are—to accept your flaws without letting them define you. To look in the mirror and say, "Yeah, I've got some sh*t, but I'm still here, and I'm still fighting." That's where your power lies. Not in perfection, but in perseverance.

So, the next time you catch yourself in the mirror, whether it's literal or figurative, take a deep breath and say this: "Mirror, mirror, f*ck you too—but I'm still here." Own your flaws, celebrate your strengths, and remember that your reflection is just that—a reflection. It doesn't define you. You define you. And that's something no mirror can ever take away.

CHAPTER NINE

Stop Apologizing for Breathing

L et me ask you something: how many times a day do you say, "I'm sorry"? If you're like most people, the number is probably higher than you think. "Sorry, I just have a quick question." "Sorry, could you move?" "Sorry, I don't mean to bother you." Hell, some of you probably apologize when *other* people bump into *you*. It's like we've been trained to feel guilty for simply existing, for taking up space, for daring to speak up or have needs. Well, f*ck that. Stop apologizing for breathing.

Let's get one thing straight: your existence isn't an inconvenience. You don't need permission to live your life, ask for what you want, or be who you are. Somewhere along the way, society decided that the polite thing to do was to shrink ourselves, to make sure we're never too loud, too bold, or too *much*. And for what? To make other people comfortable? To avoid ruffling feathers? Newsflash: no one ever changed the world—or even lived a fulfilling life—by tiptoeing around like they didn't deserve to be here.

I used to be the king of over-apologizing. Growing up in the foster care system, I learned early on that the safest thing to do was to keep my head down and not make waves. I apologized for everything, even things that weren't my fault. It was my way of surviving, of staying invisible in a world that had already decided I didn't matter. But that kind of survival mode sticks with you, even when you're no longer in danger. It becomes a habit, a reflex. And before you know it, you're apologizing for existing.

Here's the kicker: when you constantly apologize, you're sending a message—to yourself and to others—that you don't believe you're worthy. You're telling the world, "I don't deserve to take up space. I don't deserve to have needs. I don't deserve to be here." And the world will believe you. People will treat you like you're less than because you've already convinced yourself that you are.

But let me tell you something I wish someone had told me a long time ago: you have just as much right to be here as anyone else. Your voice matters. Your needs matter. You matter. And the sooner you stop apologizing for breathing, the sooner you can start living.

Of course, unlearning this sh*t isn't easy. It took me years to break the habit of over-apologizing, and even now, I catch myself slipping sometimes. But here's what helped me: every time I felt the urge to apologize for something trivial, I stopped and asked myself, "What am I really apologizing for?" Nine times out of ten, the answer was fear—fear of rejection, fear of judgment, fear of being seen as selfish or demanding. Once I recognized that, I started replacing apologies with gratitude or directness. Instead of "Sorry for asking," I'd say, "Thank you for helping me." Instead of "Sorry for being late," I'd say, "Thank you for waiting." It's a small shift, but it makes a huge difference.

Another thing I had to learn was the power of "no." For someone who grew up being told to keep quiet and comply, saying no felt like rebellion. But it's not just rebellion—it's self-respect. Every time you say no to something that doesn't align with your values or priorities, you're saying yes to yourself. And guess what? You don't owe anyone an apology for that.

Let me give you an example. When I first started writing **I Won't Break**, I had people in my life who didn't get it. They thought it was a waste of time, that I should focus on something more "practical." There were moments when their opinions got in my head, and I felt like I needed to justify myself. But then I realized something: I didn't need their approval. I didn't need to apologize for chasing something that mattered to me. So, I stopped explaining. I stopped seeking validation. And you know what? The more unapologetic I became, the more I started to believe in myself.

Now, don't get me wrong—there are times when an apology is necessary. If you hurt someone, own up to it. If you screw up, take responsibility. But don't apologize for things that aren't your fault, for having boundaries, or for being human. And definitely don't apologize for taking up space. You're not here to blend into the background or make other people comfortable. You're here to live, to grow, to create, to f*ck up and try again. You're here to take up space, unapologetically.

So, the next time you catch yourself saying, "I'm sorry" out of habit, stop. Ask yourself if an apology is really warranted. If it's not, replace it with gratitude, assertiveness, or silence. You don't owe the world an explanation for simply existing. You're not a burden, you're not a mistake, and you're not "too much." You're just enough, exactly as you are.

Stop apologizing for breathing. Breathe deeply, live boldly, and take up all the space you need. The world doesn't need another quiet, invisible soul trying not to offend anyone. The world needs *you*—loud, messy, imperfect, and unapologetically alive.

CHAPTER TEN

Love Yourself (Even If You're a Hot Mess)

Alright, let's cut the crap—self-love is hard. Especially when you're staring down the chaos of your own life, wondering how you got here and if you're ever going to get your sh*t together. Maybe your finances are a dumpster fire, your relationships are hanging by a thread, and your Google search history looks like a cry for help. Or maybe you've just had one of those weeks where nothing goes right, and you're questioning everything, including your choice of cereal. Guess what? You're not alone. You're a hot mess—and that's okay. You can still love yourself anyway.

Let's get one thing straight: self-love doesn't mean waiting until you've got your life perfectly together. It doesn't mean losing 20 pounds, landing your dream job, or magically turning into someone who never says the wrong thing in social situations. Self-love isn't a reward for being flawless—it's a practice you build while you're in the thick of your imperfections. It's about loving yourself now, not someday when you finally feel like you deserve it. Spoiler alert: you already do.

But let me be real with you: loving yourself when you feel like a walking disaster isn't easy. I've been there—hell, I've practically set up camp there at different points in my life. When I lost Caleb, when I ended up in that Texas jail cell, when I looked around at the wreckage of my life and realized I had no idea how to fix it, self-love felt like a cruel joke. How the f*ck *are you supposed to love yourself when it feels like everything you touch turns to sh*t?* Here's the answer: you love yourself *because* of that mess, not in spite of it.

Loving yourself doesn't mean ignoring your flaws or pretending everything's fine. It means accepting yourself as you are, right now, in all your messy, imperfect glory. It's looking at your life—the good, the bad, and the batsh*t crazy—and saying, "This is me. And I'm still worthy." It's about recognizing that your worth isn't tied to your achievements, your appearance, or anyone else's opinion. Your worth is non-negotiable. Period.

Now, let's talk about what self-love actually looks like. First off, it's not just bubble baths and affirmations. Sure, those things can be great, but real self-love goes deeper than that. It's about how you treat yourself when no one else is watching. It's about the way you talk to yourself when you screw up, the boundaries you set to protect your peace, and the choices you make to prioritize your well-being.

For me, learning to love myself started with unlearning all the bullsh*t I'd been told about what it means to be "worthy." Growing up, I believed I had to earn love—by being good, by achieving things, by proving my value over and over again. And when I inevitably fell short of those impossible standards, I turned that disappointment inward. I beat myself up for not being good enough, strong enough, or perfect enough. But here's the truth: love isn't something you earn. It's something you give—freely, unconditionally, and yes, even to yourself.

That doesn't mean self-love is all sunshine and rainbows. Some days, it's messy and hard. It's dragging yourself out of bed when you'd rather stay under the covers. It's forgiving yourself for that dumb thing you said in a meeting. It's choosing to eat something nourishing instead of inhaling a pint of ice cream—although let's be real, sometimes the ice cream is the right choice. Self-love is about showing up for yourself, even when you don't feel like it. Especially when you don't feel like it.

One of the hardest lessons I had to learn was that loving yourself doesn't mean you have to like everything about yourself. There are still things I wish I could change—parts of my personality, habits I'm working on, scars I carry from my past. But self-love isn't about perfection. It's about compassion. It's about looking at those parts of yourself and saying, "You're not perfect, but you're mine, and I'm going to take care of you anyway."

So, how do you start loving yourself when it feels impossible? Here are a few things that worked for me:

1. **Talk to Yourself Like Someone You Love**
    Think about the way you'd comfort a friend who's struggling. You wouldn't tear them down or call them names, would you? So why the hell do you do it to yourself? Start treating yourself with the same kindness and understanding you'd give to someone you care about.

2. **Celebrate the Small Wins**
    Self-love isn't just about big, dramatic moments of triumph. It's about recognizing the small victories—getting out of bed, brushing your teeth, choosing to try again. Those moments matter. Celebrate them.

3. **Set Boundaries Like a F*cking Boss**
    Loving yourself means protecting your energy. That means saying no to things that drain you, cutting ties with toxic people, and making time for what truly matters. It's not selfish—it's survival.

4. **Do One Thing That Brings You Joy**
    Even on the sh*ttiest days, find one thing that lights you up. Lis-

ten to your favorite song, go for a walk, watch a show that makes you laugh. Joy is an act of rebellion in a world that wants you to feel like you're not enough.

5. **Accept That You're a Work in Progress**
You're not going to wake up one day and magically have it all figured out. And that's okay. Self-love is a journey, not a destination. Give yourself permission to be a beautiful, messy work in progress.

Here's the bottom line: you don't have to wait until you've got your sh*t together to start loving yourself. In fact, the more you love yourself now, while you're still a hot mess, the easier it becomes to create the life you want. Because when you love yourself, you stop holding yourself back. You stop sabotaging your own happiness. And you start believing—really believing—that you're worthy of good things.

So, yeah, maybe you're a hot mess. Maybe your life isn't perfect, and maybe you've made some mistakes. Who the f*ck hasn't? Love yourself anyway. Love yourself because of those imperfections, not in spite of them. Because the truth is, the messiest parts of you are often the most beautiful. And when you learn to love yourself, hot mess and all, that's when the magic happens. That's when you realize you've been enough all along.

Part Three: The Joy of F*cking Up

*A*lright, let's get this out of the way: *fcking up sucks. Nobody likes to fail. Nobody enjoys screwing up so badly that you can't sleep because you're replaying the disaster in your head at 3 a.m., thinking, "Why the hell did I do that?"* But here's the secret no one tells you: your *f*ck-ups are where the real growth happens. Failure isn't the end of the road—it's the messy, pothole-filled path that leads to who you're meant to be.

This part of the book is all about reframing the way you look at failure. Instead of treating it like some big, ugly monster you need to avoid at all costs, we're going to start seeing it for what it really is: a teacher, a guide, and occasionally, a cosmic slap in the face. Because let's be honest, the lessons that stick with you the longest are the ones you learn the hard way. And if you're reading this, you've probably earned a goddamn PhD in hard lessons.

Here's the deal: nobody gets through life without *fcking up. Not me, not you, not even that perfect influencer who pretends they've got it all figured out while sipping matcha lattes on a beach. Behind every success story is a trail of failures, faceplants, and moments of, "What the actual fck was I thinking?"* The difference is, some people let their failures define them, while others use them as fuel. And you? You're going to do the latter.

In this section, we're going to dive into the beauty of *fcking up. We'll talk about why failure is inevitable, why it's necessary, and how to turn it into your biggest weapon instead of your worst enemy. You'll learn how to stop fearing failure, how to laugh at your mistakes (even the mortifying ones), and how to use every screw-up as a stepping stone to something better.*

*And yeah, I'll share some of my greatest hits in the "epic fck-ups" depart-*ment, because if I've learned one thing, it's that laughing at yourself is half the battle.

By the time we're done with this part, you'll be able to look failure in the face, flip it the bird, and say, "Thanks for the lesson." Because here's the truth: you're never going to stop *fcking up. But once you learn to em-* *brace it, you'll stop letting it hold you back. So, let's jump in and start find-* *ing the joy in your fck-ups.* After all, they're not failures—they're just practice runs for the badass you're becoming. Let's do this.

CHAPTER ELEVEN

Fail Forward, Fail Often

Failure. The word alone is enough to make most people cringe. We've been conditioned to think that failing is the ultimate sin, the one thing we should avoid at all costs. From the time we were kids, the message was drilled into us: "Don't mess up," "Play it safe," "Do it right the first time." Well, guess what? That's bullsh*t. Not only is failure inevitable, but it's also necessary. And if you're doing it right, you're going to fail a lot. The key isn't to avoid failure—it's to learn how to fail forward.

What does "fail forward" even mean? It means treating failure as a stepping stone instead of a wall. It's about taking the lesson, leaving the shame, and moving the *fck on. Because let's be real: you're going to screw up. You're going to make bad decisions, take risks that don't pay off, and have moments where you think, "Well, that was a sh*tshow."* And that's okay. The only real failure is staying stuck.

Trust me, I've failed more times than I can count. I've failed in relationships, jobs, and parenting. I've failed to keep promises, failed to rise to the occasion, and failed to be the person I wanted to be. There was the time I committed identity theft to try and create a picture-perfect life (spoiler alert: that didn't end well). Or the time I let my addiction destroy everything good in my life, thinking I could handle it on my own. Or the countless times I tried to rebuild my life, only to end up face-first in the dirt again. But here's the thing: every one of those failures taught me something. Every one of them pushed me closer to who I am today.

Failing forward isn't about pretending failure doesn't hurt. It does. It stings. Sometimes it feels like the universe is kicking you in the teeth and laughing while you bleed. But here's the kicker: failure isn't the end. It's just a detour. And if you let it, it can take you somewhere better than you ever imagined.

Here's a story that still makes me cringe and laugh at the same time. Back in my early 20s, I was dead set on building a life with Hope, my then-girlfriend. I wanted to give her everything—furniture, a nice apartment, the works. But I didn't have the money to make it happen. So, in my infinite wisdom, I decided to steal someone else's identity to get a credit line for furniture. Brilliant, right? Fast-forward a few months, and I'm in a courtroom, facing the consequences of my dumbass decision. Talk about a fail.

At the time, I felt like my life was over. I'd not only failed myself, but I'd also let down the people I cared about. But looking back, that failure taught me a lesson I desperately needed to learn: shortcuts don't work. Trying to fake your way to success only leaves you with more sh*t to clean up. That experience forced me to face my choices and start taking responsibility for my actions. It was a painful lesson, but one I wouldn't trade for anything.

So how do you fail forward? First, you've got to change the way you think about failure. Instead of seeing it as a dead end, start seeing it as a redirection. Failure isn't a sign that you're not good enough—it's a sign that you're trying. And trying is the only way to grow. Think of failure as a feedback loop. It's life's way of saying, "Not this way. Try something else."

Second, you've got to separate failure from your identity. Just because you failed doesn't mean you're a failure. Read that again. Failure is an event, not a label. It's something that happens to you, not something you are. The more you internalize that, the easier it becomes to pick yourself up and try again.

Third, laugh at your failures. Seriously. If you can't laugh at your mistakes, they'll own you. Humor is the ultimate shield against shame. Did you bomb a presentation? Laugh about how you accidentally used the word "moist" in front of a room full of executives. Did you send a drunk text to your ex? Laugh about how autocorrect turned "I miss you" into "I milk you." Own your screw-ups, find the humor, and move the hell on.

Finally, keep moving. The worst thing you can do after a failure is stand still. Action is the antidote to fear and regret. Even if you don't know exactly what to do next, take a step. Any step. Forward momentum is key. When I was sitting in that jail cell after being arrested, I had two choices: wallow in self-pity or start figuring out how to rebuild. I chose to rebuild. And yeah, it was messy and hard, but every small step I took brought me closer to the life I wanted.

Here's the truth: failure isn't optional. If you're out here living, trying, and putting yourself out there, you're going to fail. The question isn't "Will I fail?" but "How will I handle it when I do?" Will you let it stop you, or will you use it as fuel? Will you let it define you, or will you let it refine you? The choice is yours.

So, fail forward. Fail often. Fail big and loud and with your whole f*cking heart. Because every failure is a chance to grow, to learn, and to become the badass you're meant to be. And when you look back, you'll see that your so-called failures weren't failures at all—they were the building blocks of your success. Keep going. Keep trying. Keep failing. And whatever you do, don't stop.

CHAPTER TWELVE

Laugh at Your F*ck-Ups

Let's face it: *fcking up is embarrassing. You trip over your own feet, say the wrong thing at the worst possible moment, or make a decision so epically bad that even your dog looks at you like, "Really, bro?" But here's the thing—life is full of sh*tshows,* and if you can't learn to laugh at them, you're in for a miserable ride. Because let me tell you, your ability to laugh at your f*ck-ups might just be the secret weapon that keeps you sane.

We all f*ck up. It's part of being human. The sooner you accept that, the easier it gets to roll with the punches. And I don't mean those polite, uncomfortable chuckles where you're pretending to be okay while dying inside. I mean full-on belly laughs—the kind that make your sides hurt and your eyes water. Because when you can laugh at your mistakes, you take away their power. Suddenly, they're not these devastating failures hanging over your head. They're just funny stories waiting to be told at the right moment.

Take it from me, I've got enough material to host a one-man comedy show. Like the time I decided to play psychic matchmaker and gave one of my clients advice that accidentally tanked her relationship. Yep, that happened. Or the time I tried to cook a "fancy" dinner for Anthony and somehow set the kitchen on fire. Pro tip: don't put a towel on a hot stove. And then there's the crown jewel of my f*ck-ups: committing identity theft to buy furniture for my apartment because I thought it would fix my relationship with Hope. I mean, who even does that? Spoiler alert: not only did it not fix anything, but it landed me in jail. Talk about a facepalm moment.

At the time, none of these things were funny. They were stressful, humiliating, and downright painful. But looking back, I can see the humor in all of it. Because really, what else can you do? You either laugh or cry, and if you're smart, you'll pick laughter. Crying gives you puffy eyes and a headache. Laughing gives you abs. (Okay, maybe not actual abs, but it's better for you, trust me.)

So how do you start laughing at your f*ck-ups when they feel anything but funny? First, you have to stop taking yourself so damn seriously. Nobody is perfect, and nobody expects you to be—except maybe you. The truth is, people love a good self-deprecating story. It makes you relatable, approachable, and human. The next time you screw up, try telling the story as if it happened to someone else. I guarantee it'll start to sound funnier when you're not stuck in the shame spiral.

Second, put things in perspective. Ask yourself, "Will this matter in a week? A month? A year?" Most of the time, the answer is no. That cringe-worthy text you accidentally sent to your ex? Hilarious in hindsight. That awkward thing you said at the office party? Nobody remembers it except you. We spend so much energy beating ourselves up for things that don't even register on other people's radar. Let that sh*t go.

Third, find the humor in the situation. Even the darkest moments have something ridiculous in them if you look hard enough. Like the time I was sitting in that Texas jail cell, listening to my cellmate snore like a dying walrus. At first, I was pissed. But after a while, I started laughing at the absurdity of it all. Here I was, locked up for one of the dumbest decisions of my life, and my biggest problem was that I couldn't get any sleep because of this guy. It didn't change the situation, but it made it a hell of a lot easier to deal with.

Now, I'm not saying you have to laugh at every single screw-up in the moment. Sometimes, you need a little distance before the humor kicks in. And that's okay. But eventually, you'll get to a place where you can look back and think, "Damn, that was a sh*tshow—but at least it makes a good story." And honestly, isn't that what life is all about? Collecting stories to tell over drinks or at family reunions?

The beauty of laughing at your f*ck-ups is that it changes the narrative. Instead of being a victim of your mistakes, you become the hero of your own comedy. You're no longer defined by your failures—you're defined by how you handle them. And when you can laugh at yourself, you show the world that you're strong enough to roll with the punches. Plus, it's way more fun than wallowing in regret.

So, the next time you screw up—and trust me, you will—try this: take a deep breath, step back, and find the humor in it. Maybe not right away, but eventually. Because every mistake is just a story waiting to be told, and every story is a chance to laugh at how gloriously imperfect life can be. And when you can laugh at your *fck-ups, you're not just surviving—you're thriving. So go ahead, f*ck up*, laugh it off, and keep going. You've got this. And if all else fails, at least you'll have some killer stories to tell.

CHAPTER THIRTEEN

Quit Trying So Hard

Here's a revolutionary idea: stop trying so damn hard. Seriously. Quit it. I know you've been programmed to believe that if you're not busting your ass 24/7, you're falling behind. Hustle culture has brainwashed us into thinking that working harder, faster, and longer is the only way to matter. But here's the truth: trying too hard isn't noble—it's exhausting. And half the time, it's not even necessary.

The world loves to glorify overachievers. You know the type: waking up at 4 a.m., drinking green juice, hitting the gym, crushing goals before most of us have even figured out what to eat for breakfast. Good for them, I guess. But for the rest of us mortals, trying to keep up with that sh*t feels like running a marathon on a treadmill. You're working your ass off, but you're not actually getting anywhere. And let's be honest: does anyone even like green juice?

Here's the deal: trying too hard doesn't guarantee success. In fact, it often backfires. You burn out, lose focus, and forget why you were trying in the first place. Trust me, I know this firsthand. For years, I was the guy who tried way too hard to prove myself to everyone. To be the perfect partner, the perfect psychic, the perfect everything. And guess what? All it got me was a front-row seat to my own breakdown. The harder I tried, the less authentic I became. I was so busy chasing perfection that I lost sight of who I was and what I actually wanted.

Take my early career as a psychic, for example. I was obsessed with being the best. I took on too many clients, worked ridiculous hours, and bent over backward to make sure everyone was happy. I thought if I just tried hard enough, I'd earn respect and success. But all I earned was a one-way ticket to burnout. I started resenting the work, the clients, and myself. It wasn't until I stepped back and stopped overdoing it that things started to fall into place. Funny how that works.

So, why do we try so hard? For most of us, it boils down to fear. Fear of failure, fear of judgment, fear of not being enough. We think if we just work harder, achieve more, or prove ourselves, we'll finally feel worthy. But here's the secret: you're already enough. You don't need to hustle yourself into the ground to earn your place in the world. You already belong.

Now, I'm not saying you should sit on your ass and do nothing. Ambition is great, and hard work has its place. But there's a difference between working hard and working yourself into the ground. The key is to work smarter, not harder. Focus on what actually matters—what brings you joy, what aligns with your values, what moves you closer to the life you want. Everything else? Let it go.

Let's talk about letting go for a minute, because it's easier said than done. We're so wired to equate effort with worth that the idea of doing less feels like slacking off. But here's the thing: sometimes, doing less is exactly what you need. It gives you space to breathe, to reflect, and to get clear on what you actually want. It's not about giving up—it's about letting go of the sh*t that's weighing you down so you can focus on what truly matters.

For me, this looked like reevaluating my priorities. When I stopped trying to be everything to everyone, I had the energy to focus on the things that mattered most: my relationships, my health, and my creativity. I started saying no to things that didn't serve me and yes to the things that did. And you know what? The world didn't fall apart. In fact, my life got better. Go figure.

So, how do you quit trying so hard? Start by asking yourself this: "Who am I doing this for?" If the answer isn't you, it's time to rethink your approach. Next, set boundaries. Stop saying yes to every request, every opportunity, and every demand on your time. You're not a f*cking machine, and you don't owe anyone an explanation for protecting your energy. Finally, learn to let go of the need for perfection. It's okay to do your best and leave it at that. Good enough is often more than enough.

Here's the truth: life isn't a contest. There's no prize for working the hardest, trying the most, or being the busiest. The people who matter won't love you any less if you slow down. And the ones who do? They're not your people. So quit trying so hard. Take a deep breath, step back, and let life flow. You might be surprised at how much better things turn out when you're not forcing them.

At the end of the day, your worth isn't measured by how hard you try. It's measured by how authentically you live. So let go of the grind, let go of the guilt, and start focusing on what really matters. Because when you stop trying so hard, you make room for the things that truly deserve your effort—and that's where the magic happens.

CHAPTER FOURTEEN

Get Up, Dust Off, Repeat

Life is going to knock you down. Hard. It's not a question of *if*—it's *when*. You'll get sucker-punched by circumstances, blindsided by people you trusted, and sometimes, you'll trip over your own damn feet. But here's the thing: getting knocked down isn't what defines you. What defines you is how many times you get the f*ck back up. And trust me, you're going to get really good at it.

I've been knocked down more times than I can count. Life didn't just kick me; it stomped on my chest, spat in my face, and then had the audacity to laugh while I lay there wondering if I even had the strength to move. I've lost family, I've lost my son, I've lost myself more times than I care to admit. But every single time, I've gotten back up. Sometimes it wasn't pretty—hell, most times it wasn't. But I've learned that it's not about getting up gracefully. It's about getting up, period.

Let's talk about the process, because it's not some magical, Hollywood-style moment where inspiring music swells and you suddenly rise like a phoenix from the ashes. No, it's gritty, painful, and often slow as hell. Getting back up starts with a decision—a decision that, no matter how bad things are, you're not staying down. That decision doesn't come easily. It's not like you wake up one day and think, "Oh, I feel great! Let's conquer the world!" Most of the time, it's more like, "*Fck this, I'm tired of feeling like sh*t. Let's try something different."

One of the hardest times I had to get back up was after I lost Caleb. That loss hit me like a freight train, and for a long time, I didn't want to get up. I wanted to stay in the pit of my grief and guilt, wallowing in the belief that I'd failed as a father, as a person. It felt safer to stay down than to face the pain head-on. But here's the thing about staying down—it doesn't make the pain go away. It just gives it more room to grow.

Getting up doesn't mean you've got it all figured out. It doesn't mean you suddenly feel strong or ready to take on the world. It just means you're willing to take one small step forward, even if it's shaky as hell. For me, that first step was writing. Pouring my pain onto the page was messy and raw, but it was also cathartic. It didn't fix everything, but it gave me something to hold onto—a lifeline to pull myself out of the pit.

The next step is dusting yourself off. This part is tricky because it requires you to let go of the shame and self-blame that often come with falling. It's easy to beat yourself up, to dwell on all the ways you think you f*cked up. But shame doesn't serve you—it shackles you. Dusting yourself off means forgiving yourself, even when it feels impossible. It means saying, "Yeah, I screwed up, but that doesn't mean I'm screwed forever."

And then comes the part we all hate: repeating the process. Because guess what? Life isn't done knocking you down. There will be more punches, more falls, more moments where you wonder if it's even worth it. And every time, you'll have to decide to get back up again. But here's the good news: the more you do it, the stronger you become. Resilience isn't something you're born with—it's something you build, one fall and one rise at a time.

Let me give you a pro tip: don't do it alone. Getting up is easier when you've got people in your corner. Whether it's a friend, a partner, or even a therapist, having someone to lean on can make all the difference. When I was at my lowest, Anthony was my rock. He didn't try to fix me or tell me to "cheer up." He just stood by me, held space for my pain, and reminded me that I wasn't alone. Sometimes, that's all you need to start climbing out of the pit.

And let's not forget humor. Yes, even in the darkest times, you've got to find something to laugh about. Humor is what keeps you sane, what reminds you that life isn't all doom and gloom. When I was recovering from some of my worst f*ck-ups, I started looking for the absurdity in my situation. Like the time I tried to meditate to "find inner peace" and ended up falling asleep in the middle of a yoga class. Or the time I gave a psychic reading while half-asleep and accidentally predicted someone's dog was their soulmate. Laughter doesn't erase the pain, but it makes it more bearable.

So, here's the bottom line: falling isn't failure. Staying down is. Life is going to knock you on your ass, and sometimes it's going to feel like you'll never get back up. But you will. You'll take a deep breath, plant your hands on the ground, and push yourself to your feet. You'll dust yourself off, shake off the shame, and take one wobbly step forward. And when life knocks you down again, you'll do it all over. Not because it's easy, but because it's worth it.

The world doesn't need perfect people. It needs people who fall, get back up, and keep going. So when you hit the ground—and trust me, you will—remember this: get up, dust off, repeat. It's not glamorous, but it's how you survive. And eventually, it's how you thrive. Keep going. You're stronger than you think.

CHAPTER FIFTEEN

The Power of Giving Zero F*cks

Let me drop a truth bomb: most of the things you give a *fck about right now don't matter. Not even a little. Think about all the energy you've wasted worrying about what other people think, stressing over things you can't control, or bending over backward to meet expectations that aren't even yours. Exhausting, right? That's because giving too many fcks* is a one-way ticket to burnout, anxiety, and a life that doesn't feel like your own. The solution? Start giving zero f*cks—strategically, of course.

Before you freak out, let me clarify: I'm not saying you should stop caring about everything. Some things are worth your time and energy—your health, your relationships, your dreams. But most of the sh*t *you stress about? Nah. That's the noise you need to tune out. Giving zero fcks* isn't about being reckless or indifferent; it's about protecting your energy and focusing on what actually matters.

I didn't always get this. For most of my life, I was a chronic over-giver-of-fcks. *I cared about everyone's opinions—friends, family, strangers, the lady judging my grocery cart because I had six boxes of mac and cheese and no vegetables. I wanted to be liked, respected, and seen as "enough." So, I bent over backward to please everyone, even at the expense of my own happiness. Spoiler alert: it didn't work. No matter how hard I tried, someone always had something to say. And you know what? Their opinions didn't pay my bills, heal my scars, or make my life any easier. That's when I realized I was handing out fcks like free samples at Costco,* and it was draining the hell out of me.

The turning point came when I hit rock bottom. Sitting in a Texas jail cell, stripped of everything I thought made me valuable, I had nothing left to prove and no one left to impress. It was just me and my mistakes. And in that moment, something clicked: I didn't need anyone's approval to matter. The world wasn't going to stop spinning if I stopped trying to please it. So, I started rationing my f*cks. I decided that if something didn't align with my values, my peace, or my goals, it wasn't worth my energy. And let me tell you, it was the most liberating decision I've ever made.

Here's the thing about giving zero *fcks: it's not about being selfish—it's about being selective. You only have so much time and energy in a day, so why waste it on sh*t that doesn't serve you? Every fck you give is an investment, and if you're not getting a return on that investment, it's time to pull the plug. Stop overthinking the little things, like whether your outfit is "on trend" or if your neighbor is judging your lawn. Spoiler: they're not. They're too busy worrying about their own sh*t.*

Of course, learning to give zero f*cks isn't easy. It takes practice, especially if you've spent your whole life caring too much. The first step is figuring out what truly matters to you. Ask yourself: "What do I actually care about? What brings me joy? What aligns with the life I want to build?" Once you know the answers, start cutting out anything that doesn't make the list. If it's not adding value to your life, it's not worth your energy.

Second, set some f*cking boundaries. Stop saying yes to every request, every invite, every demand on your time. You don't owe anyone an explanation for protecting your peace. And if someone can't respect your boundaries? That's a them problem, not a you problem. Remember, "no" is a complete sentence.

Third, stop giving a f*ck about things you can't control. This one's a game-changer. You can't control other people's opinions, the weather, or the fact that your favorite show got canceled. So why stress over it? Focus on what you *can* control—your choices, your reactions, your mindset. Let go of the rest.

Now, let's talk about the magic that happens when you start giving zero f*cks. First off, you'll have so much more energy. Instead of wasting it on pointless worries and people-pleasing, you can channel it into things that actually matter. Your goals, your relationships, your well-being. Second, you'll feel lighter—like a weight has been lifted off your shoulders. Because when you stop caring about what doesn't matter, you make room for what does.

But the best part? You'll feel free. Free to live your life on your own terms, without constantly second-guessing yourself or worrying about what other people think. You'll realize that most of the judgment you feared was never real—it was just a story you told yourself. And even if someone does judge you? Who gives a f*ck? Their opinion doesn't define you.

Here's the bottom line: you don't have to carry the weight of the world on your shoulders. You don't have to please everyone, meet every expectation, or worry about every little thing. Life is too short to waste on sh*t *that doesn't matter. So, take a deep breath, let go of the noise, and start giving zero f*cks* about the things that don't serve you. You'll be amazed at how much lighter, freer, and happier you feel.

And if someone has a problem with that? Well, you already know the answer: zero f*cks given. Keep doing you.

Part Four: The Freedom of Realness

Here's the thing: we spend so much of our lives trying to be someone we're not. We slap on masks, chase expectations, and twist ourselves into knots trying to fit into molds we didn't even agree to. And for what? Approval? Validation? A gold star from people who probably don't give a sh*t *anyway? It's exhausting. But you know what's not? Being real. There's a kind of freedom that comes with owning your truth, letting go of the fake sh*t,* and showing up as your messy, imperfect, gloriously authentic self. That's what this part of the book is all about.

Realness isn't just about being honest with others—it's about being honest with yourself. It's about stripping away the filters, the facades, and the bullsh*t and getting down to who you really are. What do you value? What do you want? What makes your soul light up? These aren't easy questions to answer, especially when you've spent years living for everyone but yourself. But trust me, the journey is worth it.

In this section, we're going to talk about what it means to live a real, unfiltered life. We'll dive into the power of defining success on your own terms, why happiness is overrated (and peace is better), and how to build relationships that thrive on honesty instead of pretense. We'll also tackle the hard stuff, like how to let go of people who can't handle your truth and why embracing your flaws is the key to self-acceptance. And yeah, we're going to laugh along the way, because if you can't laugh at the absurdity of it all, what's the point?

Realness is scary at first. It feels vulnerable, exposed, and risky. But once you step into it, you'll wonder why you wasted so much time pretending. There's a kind of freedom that comes with saying, "This is me—take it or leave it." And spoiler alert: the right people will always take it. So, let's dive in and explore the messy, beautiful, liberating freedom of being unapologetically real. Ready? Let's go.

CHAPTER SIXTEEN

Define Success for Your Damn Self

Let me hit you with some cold, hard truth: most people's definition of success is absolute bullsh*t. *Society tells us that success looks like a six-figure income, a house with a white picket fence, a fancy job title, and 2.5 kids who are probably named something trendy like Asher or Quinn. And while there's nothing wrong with wanting those things if they genuinely light your soul on fire, here's the kicker: if you're chasing them because you think you're supposed to, you're running someone else's race. And let me tell you, that sh*t is exhausting.*

Here's the thing about success: it's not one-size-fits-all. What feels like "making it" to one person might feel like a prison to someone else. For years, I chased what I thought success was supposed to look like. I wanted the perfect relationship, the perfect career, the perfect life. I thought if I could just tick all the right boxes, I'd finally feel like I mattered. Spoiler alert: I ticked some of those boxes, and I still felt empty as hell. That's because success isn't about the boxes—it's about what actually matters to *you*.

Take a second and ask yourself: what does success mean to me? Not to your parents, your friends, your Instagram followers—*you*. Does it mean climbing the corporate ladder? Starting your own business? Traveling the world? Maybe it's something simpler, like spending more time with your family or finally learning how to cook without setting off the smoke alarm. Whatever it is, own it. Because the second you stop letting other people define your goals, you'll start to feel something you probably haven't felt in a while: freedom.

For me, redefining success was a long, messy process. After losing Caleb, my entire world fell apart. I felt like I'd failed at the one thing that mattered most: being a father. Everything I'd been chasing suddenly seemed meaningless. I hit rock bottom, and in that darkness, I started to ask myself some hard questions: What do I actually want? What kind of life would make me feel whole? What does "enough" look like for me? The answers weren't easy, but they were real. And they were mine.

Here's what I realized: for me, success isn't about a fancy house or a fat bank account. It's about peace. It's about waking up in the morning and feeling good about who I am and how I'm living. It's about the relationships I've built, the impact I've had, and the joy I've found in the little things—like cooking breakfast with Anthony or walking my dogs through the New Mexico desert. That's my definition of success, and it's worth more to me than any paycheck or trophy ever could be.

Now, let's get practical. How do you define success for yourself when you've spent your whole life chasing someone else's dream? First, get clear on your values. What matters most to you? Is it freedom? Stability? Creativity? Connection? Once you know your values, you can start building a life that aligns with them. Second, stop comparing yourself to others. Your journey is yours, and comparing it to someone else's highlight reel is a surefire way to feel like sh*t. Third, set goals that actually excite you. Not the goals you think you *should* have, but the ones that light a fire in your gut.

And here's the most important part: be flexible. Your definition of success will evolve as you do, and that's okay. What matters is that you keep checking in with yourself and making sure you're still on a path that feels right for you. Because the second your definition of success stops feeling like freedom and starts feeling like a trap, it's time to reevaluate.

Let me give you a personal example. For years, I thought success meant being the best psychic I could be—taking on as many clients as possible, building a reputation, making a name for myself. And for a while, it felt good. But eventually, I started to feel burned out. I realized that what I actually wanted wasn't more clients or more recognition—it was more time to write, to reflect, to just *be*. So I shifted gears, cut back on work, and focused on the things that truly brought me joy. And guess what? The world didn't end. In fact, my life got better.

The point is, success isn't about reaching some mythical finish line. It's about building a life that feels good to live. It's about knowing what matters to you and having the courage to go after it, even if it doesn't look like what everyone else is doing. And yeah, it takes guts to step off the hamster wheel and say, "No thanks, I'm doing this my way." But trust me, it's worth it.

So, define success for your damn self. Write your own rules, chase your own dreams, and let go of the sh*t that doesn't serve you. Because at the end of the day, the only person who gets to decide if you're successful is you. And when you build a life that feels good on your terms, that's the kind of success no one can take away.

CHAPTER SEVENTEEN

Happiness Is Overrated

Let me say something that might sound crazy at first: happiness is overrated. Yeah, I said it. This constant chase for happiness—the picture-perfect, Instagram-filtered kind—has us all f*cked up. We've been sold this idea that happiness is the ultimate goal, the finish line we should all be sprinting toward. But here's the truth: happiness is fleeting, unpredictable, and, quite frankly, not all it's cracked up to be.

Don't get me wrong—happiness is great. It's that warm, fuzzy feeling when things are going right, when you're laughing with friends, or when your dog does something stupidly adorable. But here's the problem: we treat happiness like it's a permanent state, like we've failed if we're not walking around with a constant sh*t-eating grin. Newsflash: no one is happy all the time. Not even the people who seem to have it all figured out. And chasing that unrealistic version of happiness is a recipe for misery.

Here's the thing about happiness: it's a feeling, not a destination. And like every other feeling—anger, sadness, excitement—it's temporary. It comes and goes. Trying to hold onto happiness 24/7 is like trying to catch smoke with your bare hands. You can't do it, and the harder you try, the more frustrated you'll get.

What if I told you there's something better than happiness? Something deeper, more stable, and more fulfilling? It's called peace. Unlike happiness, peace doesn't depend on external circumstances. It's not about what's happening around you—it's about what's happening within you. Peace is waking up in the morning and feeling okay, even if life isn't perfect. It's knowing that you can handle whatever comes your way, that you're grounded, that you're enough. And let me tell you, peace is way more valuable than some fleeting high of happiness.

I learned this the hard way. For years, I thought happiness was the goal. I chased it in all the wrong places—relationships, work, even material things. I told myself, "If I can just get this, then I'll be happy." But every time I got what I thought I wanted, the happiness wore off. The newness faded. And I was left feeling empty again, like I was back at square one. It wasn't until I hit rock bottom—when I lost Caleb, when I found myself in jail, when I had nothing left to lose—that I realized I'd been chasing the wrong thing. Happiness didn't save me. Peace did.

So, how do you stop chasing happiness and start finding peace? First, let go of the idea that life is supposed to be all sunshine and rainbows. It's not. Life is messy, unpredictable, and sometimes downright cruel. But it's also beautiful, meaningful, and full of opportunities for growth. The key is to stop fighting the bad moments and start embracing the whole picture—the highs, the lows, and everything in between.

Second, focus on what you can control. A lot of our unhappiness comes from trying to change things that are out of our hands—other people's opinions, the past, the weather. But peace comes from accepting what you can't change and focusing on what you can. Your mindset, your choices, your reactions—that's where your power lies.

Third, stop measuring your life by how happy you are. Instead, ask yourself: Am I living in alignment with my values? Am I showing up as the person I want to be? Am I finding meaning in the things I do? Because meaning lasts longer than happiness. Meaning gives you something to hold onto, even when sh*t hits the fan.

Finally, practice gratitude. I know, I know—gratitude can feel like one of those self-help buzzwords that people throw around without meaning it. But hear me out. Gratitude doesn't mean ignoring your struggles or pretending everything's fine. It means choosing to notice the good in your life, even when things are hard. It's not about forcing yourself to be happy—it's about finding peace in the present moment.

Let me give you an example. After losing Caleb, I didn't think I'd ever feel happy again. The grief was so overwhelming, it felt like it would swallow me whole. But over time, I started to find little moments of peace. Sitting outside with Anthony, watching the dogs play, feeling the sun on my face—it didn't erase the pain, but it gave me a sense of calm. It reminded me that life is still worth living, even when it's not perfect. And that peace? That's what carried me through.

So, yeah, happiness is nice. But it's not the be-all, end-all of life. Stop chasing it like it's the only thing that matters. Instead, focus on building a life that feels meaningful, authentic, and peaceful. Because when you find peace, you'll realize that happiness isn't something you have to chase—it's something that shows up naturally, in its own time, as a byproduct of a life well-lived.

And when it does show up? Enjoy the hell out of it. Laugh, dance, take a million pictures. But don't cling to it. Let it come and go, like every other feeling, knowing that your peace is what truly sustains you. Because at the end of the day, happiness is fleeting—but peace? Peace is forever.

CHAPTER EIGHTEEN

Love, but Don't Lose Yourself

Love. The word alone can make your heart race or your stomach churn, depending on your experience. It's one of the most powerful things in life—capable of healing, inspiring, and tearing you apart all at once. And while love can be beautiful, it also has a sneaky way of pulling you into a trap if you're not careful. The trap? Losing yourself.

Here's the thing: love is supposed to add to your life, not consume it. It's not about disappearing into someone else's world, someone else's needs, or someone else's definition of who you should be. But too often, we forget that. We bend, twist, and contort ourselves trying to be what we think our partner wants. And before we know it, we're staring in the mirror at a stranger, wondering, "Where the hell did I go?"

Trust me, I've been there. When I was with Hope, I thought love meant doing whatever it took to make her happy. I ignored my own needs, silenced my own voice, and even crossed legal boundaries (hello, identity theft) to create a life I thought would impress her. Spoiler alert: it didn't work. Instead of building a stronger relationship, I built resentment—toward her, toward myself, and toward the illusion of love I was chasing. I lost myself in that relationship, and it took hitting rock bottom to realize that love isn't about giving all of yourself away. It's about showing up as your whole self and being loved for exactly that.

So, how do you love without losing yourself? First, you have to know who the f*ck you are. This sounds obvious, but a lot of people jump into relationships without a solid sense of self. They rely on their partner to define their worth, their identity, and their happiness. But here's the truth: you can't pour from an empty cup. If you don't love yourself first, you'll end up looking for validation in your partner—and that's a recipe for disaster.

Second, set boundaries. This is where a lot of people struggle, especially in relationships. We're taught that love means sacrifice, that it's noble to put your partner's needs above your own. And while compromise is important, there's a big difference between compromise and self-abandonment. Boundaries aren't walls—they're guideposts that help you protect your peace, your values, and your sense of self. If your partner can't respect your boundaries, that's a red flag, not a love story.

Third, keep your own life. It's easy to get swept up in the excitement of a new relationship or the comfort of a long-term one, but don't forget to maintain your own interests, friendships, and goals. Love isn't about becoming one person—it's about being two whole people who choose to share their lives. If you give up everything that makes you *you*, what are you really bringing to the table?

Let me share something personal. When I met Anthony, I was terrified of repeating old patterns. I didn't want to lose myself again. So, I made a promise to myself: I would love him with everything I had, but I wouldn't abandon myself in the process. And you know what? He loved me even more for it. Our relationship isn't perfect—no relationship is—but it's built on mutual respect, honesty, and the understanding that we're both individuals first. He loves me for who I am, not for what I sacrifice to make him happy. And that's the kind of love everyone deserves.

Of course, loving without losing yourself isn't always easy. There will be moments when you're tempted to over-give, to over-compromise, to make yourself smaller for the sake of harmony. In those moments, remember this: love that requires you to disappear isn't love—it's control, codependency, or insecurity masquerading as love. Real love doesn't ask you to give up your identity. It celebrates it.

Here's a practical exercise: write down a list of things that make you feel like you. Maybe it's painting, hiking, hanging out with friends, or binge-watching terrible reality TV. Whatever it is, commit to keeping those things in your life, even when you're in a relationship. If your partner can't support that, they're not the right person for you.

And let's talk about self-love for a second, because it's the foundation of everything. Loving yourself isn't selfish—it's necessary. When you love yourself, you set the standard for how others should treat you. You're less likely to tolerate toxic behavior, less likely to compromise your values, and less likely to lose yourself in someone else's shadow. Self-love isn't just a nice idea—it's a survival skill.

So, here's the bottom line: love fiercely, but don't forget who you are. Protect your sense of self like your life depends on it—because in a way, it does. The best relationships are built on authenticity, not sacrifice. When you show up as your whole self, you give your partner permission to do the same. And that? That's real love.

Love deeply. Love honestly. But most importantly, love yourself enough to never disappear. Because the world doesn't need another person who's lost themselves in the name of love. The world needs you—whole, real, and unapologetically you.

CHAPTER NINETEEN

The Family You Choose

Let's get real: not everyone gets the family they deserve. Maybe your biological family is supportive and loving, and if that's the case, you're one of the lucky ones. But for a lot of us, family is complicated. Sometimes, the people who are supposed to love us unconditionally are the ones who hurt us the most. Sometimes, they're the reason we're carrying so much damn baggage in the first place. And while you can't change the family you're born into, you *can* choose the family you build.

Here's the thing: family isn't just about blood. It's about connection, trust, and the people who show up for you when sh*t hits the fan. It's about the ones who see you for who you really are and love you anyway. The ones who hold space for your pain, celebrate your wins, and stick around even when you're not at your best. That's what family is supposed to feel like, and if you didn't get that from the people you share DNA with, you're not alone. But you're also not stuck. Because the family you choose can be just as powerful—if not more so—than the one you were born into.

For me, family has always been a loaded word. Growing up in the foster care system, I didn't have the safety net of parents or siblings to fall back on. My "family" was a revolving door of strangers—some kind, some not—who weren't really mine. That kind of instability messes with your head. It made me think I didn't deserve love or stability. It made me believe I had to earn my place in someone's life. And for a long time, I let those beliefs dictate how I saw myself and my relationships.

But here's what I've learned: family isn't something you're given—it's something you create. It's built through love, loyalty, and shared experiences. It's the friend who picks up the phone at 2 a.m. when you're falling apart. It's the partner who sees your scars and says, "I love you even more because of them." It's the community you build around yourself—the people who remind you that you're never truly alone.

Take Anthony, for example. He's my chosen family in every sense of the word. When I met him, I was still piecing myself back together from years of trauma and bad decisions. I wasn't whole—I was a walking patchwork of scars and hope. But he didn't flinch. He didn't try to fix me or change me. He just showed up, day after day, with love and patience and the kind of quiet strength I didn't know I needed. He became my anchor, my home, my family.

And then there are my friends—the ones who've stuck with me through the chaos, the ones who've seen me at my lowest and still believed in me. They're not just friends; they're my tribe. They're the people who remind me that family isn't about obligation—it's about choice. And every time they choose me, I'm reminded that I'm worthy of love and connection, no matter how broken I've felt in the past.

But let me be clear: building a chosen family doesn't mean cutting off your biological family completely (unless that's what you need to do for your own well-being—no judgment here). It's about expanding your definition of family to include the people who truly make you feel seen, safe, and loved. It's about letting go of the guilt and shame that come with traditional ideas of family and embracing the freedom to create your own.

So, how do you find your chosen family? Start by looking for people who align with your values and energy. These are the ones who uplift you, challenge you to grow, and love you without conditions. They're the ones who make you feel like you can exhale—like you don't have to perform or pretend to belong. When you find those people, hold onto them. Nurture those relationships. Show up for them the way they show up for you.

And here's the kicker: being part of a chosen family isn't just about what you get—it's about what you give. It's about being the friend who listens without judgment, the partner who loves fiercely, the person who creates a safe space for others to be themselves. Family is a two-way street, and the more love and energy you pour into it, the more you'll get back.

Let me leave you with this: your chosen family is proof that you're not alone. No matter how broken your past feels, no matter how many times you've been let down or abandoned, you have the power to create a new kind of family—one built on love, trust, and mutual respect. It's not about replacing the family you were born into; it's about expanding your heart to include the people who truly deserve a place in it.

So go out there and find your tribe. Build your family, brick by brick, with the people who make you feel whole. And remember: the family you choose is just as valid, just as real, and just as powerful as the one you were born into. Maybe even more so.

CHAPTER TWENTY

Keep It Real, Even When It's Ugly

*L*et's not sugarcoat this: life can get really *fcking ugly. And when it does, the temptation to fake it—pretend you're fine, slap on a smile, and act like everything's peachy—is strong as hell. But let me save you some time: faking it doesn't work. Not for long, anyway. You can't heal what you're not willing to face. You can't grow if you're too busy pretending to be perfect. The only way to get through the ugly sh*t is to keep it real, no matter how messy or uncomfortable it gets.

We live in a world obsessed with appearances. Social media, reality TV, even casual conversations are drenched in this weird, unspoken rule: never let anyone see you sweat. But here's the problem with that: it's bullsh*t. Nobody has it all together. Not you, not me, not that influencer with the perfect aesthetic and a thousand sponsored posts. Life is messy, and hiding that mess doesn't make it go away. If anything, it just makes you feel more alone.

Take it from me, I've spent more time than I'd like to admit pretending to be fine when I was anything but. Growing up in foster care, I learned early on that showing vulnerability was dangerous. If people knew you were struggling, they'd either pity you or use it against you. So, I got really good at acting like everything was okay, even when my world was falling apart. And for a while, it worked. Until it didn't.

One of my lowest points was after losing Caleb. That kind of pain doesn't just break you—it shatters you. And instead of letting myself grieve, I tried to power through it. I threw myself into distractions, told everyone I was "fine," and buried the hurt so deep I almost convinced myself it wasn't there. But the thing about pain is, it doesn't just disappear because you ignore it. It sits there, festering, waiting for you to deal with it. And if you don't? It'll find a way to deal with you.

For me, that meant hitting rock bottom—literally and emotionally. I landed in jail, stripped of everything I thought made me valuable, and had no choice but to face the ugly truth: I was broken, angry, and lost. And as much as it sucked to admit that, it was also the first step toward healing. Because once you strip away the pretense, once you stop pretending and start being real, you give yourself permission to heal.

So, how do you keep it real when everything in you wants to fake it? First, stop running from the truth. Whatever it is—pain, fear, anger, shame—acknowledge it. Name it. Own it. Pretending it's not there doesn't make it go away. In fact, it gives it more power. When you face it head-on, you take back control.

Second, find your people. You don't have to share your mess with everyone—hell, most people won't know what to do with it. But find the ones who can handle it, the ones who love you enough to sit with you in your pain without trying to fix it. For me, that person was Anthony. He didn't try to cheer me up or tell me to "look on the bright side." He just held space for my grief, my anger, and my ugly truths. And that kind of unconditional support? It's priceless.

Third, give yourself grace. Being real doesn't mean having all the answers. It doesn't mean "getting over it" or magically fixing everything. It means showing up, even when it's hard, and being honest about where you are. It means saying, "I'm not okay, but I'm here, and I'm trying." And that's enough.

Finally, learn to laugh at the absurdity of it all. Because let's be honest: life's messiest moments are often its funniest. Like the time I tried to meditate in a yoga class to "find my center" and ended up snoring so loud I got kicked out. Or the time I gave a psychic reading while hungover and accidentally told someone their dog was their spirit guide. Keeping it real means embracing the ridiculousness of life, even when it feels like everything's falling apart.

Here's the truth: the more you try to hide the ugly parts of your life, the more isolated you'll feel. But when you let yourself be real—when you share your mess, your struggles, and your scars—you create space for connection, healing, and growth. You remind yourself (and others) that it's okay to be imperfect. It's okay to struggle. It's okay to not have it all figured out.

So, keep it real. Even when it's messy. Even when it's uncomfortable. Even when it's ugly as hell. Because realness is where the magic happens. It's where you find strength, resilience, and the kind of connection that makes life worth living. And if someone can't handle your realness? That's their loss, not yours.

Remember, the ugly parts of your story are just as important as the beautiful ones. They're what make you human, what make you relatable, and what make your journey unique. So own them. Embrace them. And keep showing up, exactly as you are. Because realness isn't just freeing—it's f*cking powerful.

Part Five: Laugh Loud, Live Wild

Life is too damn short to take it so seriously. Let's face it: no one's getting out alive, and if we're all just here for a limited time, why the hell aren't we laughing more? Why aren't we living louder, bolder, and wilder? That's what this part of the book is all about—ditching the constant stress and overthinking, and diving headfirst into the chaos, joy, and ridiculousness that makes life worth living.

This isn't about being reckless or irresponsible. It's about giving yourself permission to loosen the *fck up. It's about finding the humor in the sh*tstorms, embracing the unpredictable, and saying "yes" to the things that scare and excite you in equal measure. Because when you stop trying to control every little detail, you leave room for the magic to happen.

In this section, we're going to explore the art of not taking yourself too seriously, the power of saying "f*ck it" and going after what you want, and why some of life's best moments happen when you stop playing it safe. We'll talk about how to let go of perfection, find joy in the absurd, and create memories you'll actually want to relive (or laugh at, years down the line).

Laugh loud. Live wild. This isn't a suggestion—it's a survival strategy. Because when you let yourself fully embrace the messy, unpredictable beauty of life, you don't just survive—you thrive. So let's raise some hell, break a few rules, and rediscover the freedom of living life unapologetically. Ready? Let's go.

CHAPTER TWENTY ONE

Life's a Joke, Laugh Anyway

Here's the cold, hard truth: life is ridiculous. It's messy, unpredictable, and full of sh*t you couldn't make up if you tried. One minute, you're cruising along like you've got it all figured out, and the next, you're knee-deep in chaos wondering, "Is this really my life right now?" Spoiler alert: yes, it is. But here's the thing—if you don't learn to laugh at it, you'll spend most of your time crying. And frankly, laughing is way more fun.

Let me be clear: laughing at life doesn't mean ignoring the hard stuff. It's not about plastering on a fake smile and pretending everything's fine when it's not. It's about finding the humor in the absurdity of it all. It's about realizing that sometimes, life is such a hot mess that all you can do is throw your hands up, laugh your ass off, and roll with it. Because if you can't laugh at life, you're giving it way too much power over you.

Take my life, for example. I've had more than my fair share of WTF moments. From getting arrested for stealing credit to buy furniture (seriously, what was I thinking?) to losing everything I thought defined me, life has thrown me curveball after curveball. And yeah, there were times when I wanted to crawl under a rock and never come out. But looking back, some of those moments were so absurd, they're almost funny—emphasis on *almost*. Like the time I was sitting in that Texas jail cell, listening to my cellmate snore like a dying chainsaw, thinking, "Well, this is rock bottom." It wasn't funny then, but now? Comedy gold.

The truth is, life has a twisted sense of humor, and if you don't learn to laugh along with it, you're going to miss the joke. Like when your car breaks down on the one day you actually left the house on time. Or when your dog eats the one thing you told yourself to keep out of reach. Or when you trip over absolutely nothing in front of a group of people you were trying to impress. These moments aren't tragedies—they're punchlines. And the faster you learn to see them that way, the lighter your life will feel.

Now, I know what you're thinking: "Sure, Derrick, it's easy to laugh at the little stuff. But what about the big sh*t? *The heartbreaks, the losses, the times when life really f*cks you over?*" Trust me, I get it. There's nothing funny about losing someone you love or watching your life fall apart. But even in those dark moments, humor can be a lifeline. It doesn't erase the pain, but it gives you a reason to keep going. It reminds you that not everything is terrible all the time. Sometimes, even in the middle of your worst days, life throws you a moment so absurd, you can't help but laugh.

Let me tell you a story. After Caleb was taken from me, I didn't think I'd ever laugh again. The grief was suffocating, and every day felt like a battle just to get out of bed. But one day, in the middle of my pity party, my dog decided to go full-on Tasmanian Devil and knock over a plate of spaghetti I'd just made. The sauce went everywhere—on the walls, on me, even on the dog. I sat there, staring at the chaos, and for some reason, I started laughing. Like, really laughing. It was the first time I'd felt anything close to joy in weeks. And in that moment, I realized that even in the darkest times, life has a way of surprising you.

Here's the takeaway: life is a joke, and the punchlines are everywhere if you're willing to look for them. That doesn't mean you have to laugh at everything right away—some sh*t takes time. But when you can step back and find the humor in your situation, even the hard stuff starts to feel a little lighter.

So how do you start laughing at life when it feels like a never-ending sh*tshow? First, stop taking yourself so damn seriously. Nobody has it all figured out, and nobody expects you to, either. Second, learn to find the absurdity in your situation. Even when things go wrong, there's almost always something ridiculous about it. Third, surround yourself with people who know how to laugh. The kind of friends who can turn your worst days into funny stories and remind you not to sweat the small stuff.

And finally, give yourself permission to laugh. It's okay to find humor in the chaos, even when things are hard. It doesn't mean you're not taking life seriously—it means you're choosing to find joy in the mess. And if anyone judges you for that? F*ck 'em. They're probably just mad because they forgot how to laugh at themselves.

At the end of the day, life is a series of ups, downs, and sideways sh*tshows. *You can either let it break you or let it entertain you. So, take a deep breath, embrace the chaos, and laugh your f*cking ass off.* Because if life's going to be a joke, you might as well be in on it.

CHAPTER TWENTY TWO

Dance in the Storm

Let's get real: life doesn't always wait for sunny skies to throw you a curveball. Sometimes, the storm hits, and it feels like you're stuck in a hurricane with no umbrella, no shelter, and definitely no plan. The rain's pouring, the wind's howling, and you're standing there thinking, "Why the hell is this happening to me?" But here's the thing: you can't outrun the storm, and you sure as sh*t can't control it. What you *can* do is learn how to dance in it.

Dancing in the storm isn't about pretending the storm doesn't exist. It's not about plastering on a fake smile and saying, "Everything's fine!" when it's clearly not. It's about embracing the chaos, finding moments of joy and strength in the middle of it, and deciding that even when life is messy and unpredictable, you're still going to live fully. Because here's the truth: storms aren't permanent. The rain eventually stops, the clouds part, and the sun comes back. The question is, what kind of person do you want to be when it does?

For most of my life, I thought surviving the storm meant hunkering down, shutting everything out, and waiting for it to pass. When I lost Caleb, that's exactly what I did. I curled up in my grief, let the storm rage around me, and told myself I'd come out the other side when it was over. But you know what? That storm didn't go away on its own. I had to get up, step into the rain, and figure out how to live again—even when it felt impossible. And in doing that, I learned that the storm wasn't just something to endure. It was something to grow from.

Dancing in the storm means finding moments of joy and beauty, even when everything feels like it's falling apart. It's laughing through the tears, singing off-key in the middle of chaos, and saying, "F*ck it, I'm still here." It's not about denying the pain—it's about refusing to let it steal every ounce of light from your life. Because the storm will pass, but the strength you build while dancing in it? That stays with you forever.

So, how do you dance in the storm when everything inside you just wants to give up? First, let yourself feel the rain. Too many of us spend our lives trying to avoid discomfort, numbing ourselves to the pain with distractions, substances, or toxic positivity. But the only way to get through the storm is to feel it. Let the rain hit you. Cry if you need to. Scream if you have to. But don't run from it. The storm is part of your story, and it's shaping you in ways you can't see yet.

Second, look for small moments of joy. When the world feels like it's falling apart, joy can feel like a rebellious act. But those little sparks—a stupid meme that makes you laugh, a song that makes you want to dance, a quiet moment with someone you love—are what keep you grounded. They're proof that even in the middle of the storm, there's still beauty to be found.

Third, move your body. I don't care if it's actual dancing, a walk in the rain, or punching a pillow until you're out of breath. Moving your body reminds you that you're alive, that you're capable, and that you can still take action even when life feels overwhelming. When I was at my lowest, music became my lifeline. Blasting my favorite songs and dancing like a maniac in my living room didn't solve my problems, but it reminded me that I still had a spark left—and that was enough to keep going.

Finally, remind yourself that storms don't last forever. I know that sounds cliché, but it's true. No matter how dark and endless it feels, the storm will pass. And when it does, you'll look back and see how much stronger you've become because of it. You'll see that the rain didn't wash you away—it helped you grow.

Let me tell you a story. When I was at my rock bottom, sitting in that Texas jail cell, I felt like the storm would never end. I'd lost everything—my son, my freedom, my sense of self. But in the middle of that darkness, I found something unexpected: a glimmer of hope. It came in the form of a letter from someone I loved, reminding me that I still had a reason to fight. That glimmer didn't fix everything, but it gave me the courage to stand up, take a deep breath, and start rebuilding. And every step I've taken since then has been my way of dancing in the storm.

So, the next time life throws you into a hurricane, don't waste your energy trying to stop the rain. Embrace it. Let it soak you to the bone, let it teach you what you're made of, and then find your rhythm. Dance like no one's watching—or like everyone's watching and you don't give a f*ck. Because the storm doesn't define you. How you show up in it does.

The rain will stop. The clouds will clear. And when they do, you'll be stronger, braver, and more alive than ever. Until then, keep dancing. Keep laughing. Keep living. Because storms are temporary, but your spirit? That's unbreakable.

CHAPTER TWENTY THREE

Do It Scared

Here's a hard pill to swallow: fear isn't going anywhere. It doesn't matter how brave you are, how much self-help sh*t you read, or how many pep talks you give yourself in the mirror—fear is part of the deal. It's going to show up, whispering in your ear, telling you all the reasons you shouldn't try, shouldn't risk, shouldn't dream. And guess what? You're going to do it anyway. Because the secret isn't to wait until the fear is gone—it's to do it scared.

Let's get one thing straight: courage isn't the absence of fear. It's taking action *despite* it. It's staring your fear in the face and saying, "I see you, I feel you, and I'm still doing this." Fear doesn't mean you're weak. Fear means you're stepping out of your comfort zone, pushing your limits, and doing something that matters. And if that doesn't scare you, you're not aiming big enough.

I've spent a good chunk of my life paralyzed by fear. Fear of rejection. Fear of failure. Fear of being seen for who I really am. It showed up in all kinds of ways—making me second-guess myself, hold back, and settle for less than I deserved. But here's what I've learned: fear doesn't go away just because you hide from it. It shrinks when you face it. It fades when you take action. And sometimes, the only way out of fear is straight through it.

One of the scariest decisions I ever made was to write **I Won't Break**. I knew putting my story out there—every raw, unfiltered, messy detail—was going to open me up to judgment, criticism, and vulnerability. But I also knew that my story could help someone else feel less alone. So, I did it scared. And guess what? The fear didn't disappear overnight. I hit "publish" with my heart racing and my stomach in knots. But I did it. And the pride I felt afterward? That was worth every moment of fear.

So, how do you do it scared? First, stop waiting for the fear to go away. Fear is a normal part of the process, especially when you're doing something meaningful. If you wait for the perfect moment when you feel 100% ready and fearless, you'll never take the leap. Instead, acknowledge the fear and do the damn thing anyway.

Second, break it down. Fear thrives on overwhelm. When you're staring at the big picture, it can feel impossible. But when you break it into smaller steps, it becomes manageable. Want to start a new career? Don't focus on the giant leap—focus on sending one email, updating your resume, or researching options. Each small step chips away at the fear.

Third, flip the script. Instead of asking, "What if I fail?" ask, "What if I don't try?" Fear loves to magnify the risks, but it conveniently ignores the cost of staying stuck. What's scarier: trying and failing, or never trying and living with the regret?

And finally, remind yourself of the times you've done it scared before. Because you have. Whether it was taking that first step after a breakup, speaking up in a meeting, or trying something new, you've faced fear and survived. Let those moments remind you that you're stronger than you think.

Doing it scared doesn't mean the fear magically disappears. Your hands might still shake, your voice might still quiver, and your mind might still race with doubts. But every time you act in spite of that fear, you prove to yourself that it doesn't own you. You reclaim your power, one brave step at a time.

Let me leave you with this: fear is a sign you're on the edge of growth. It's a signal that you're stepping into something bigger than you've been before. So, instead of running from it, embrace it. Let it remind you that you're alive, you're trying, and you're doing the work. And when you look back, you'll realize that the things you did scared were the things that mattered most.

The fear isn't going anywhere. But neither are you. So take a deep breath, feel the fear, and do it scared. You've got this.

CHAPTER TWENTY FOUR

Celebrate Every Damn Thing

Celebration isn't just for birthdays, weddings, and New Year's Eve. It's for getting through a Monday without losing your sh*t. It's for finally tackling that pile of laundry that's been mocking you for weeks. It's for waking up, breathing, and deciding to show up for your life, even when it feels like the universe is conspiring against you. The truth is, life is hard enough without waiting for monumental achievements to pop bottles and throw confetti. If you want to survive—and thrive—you need to learn to celebrate every damn thing.

Let's start with why celebration matters. Celebration isn't just about patting yourself on the back—it's about building momentum. Every time you take a moment to acknowledge a win, no matter how small, you remind yourself that progress is happening. You remind yourself that you're capable, resilient, and worthy of good things. And that reminder? It's fuel. It's what keeps you going when the road ahead looks long as hell and full of potholes.

Now, I know what you're thinking: "What if there's nothing to celebrate?" Listen, there's always something. Did you get out of bed today? Celebrate that. Did you manage not to flip off that a**hole who cut you off in traffic? Toast to your self-control. Did you survive another day without completely losing your mind? That's worth a damn parade.

The point is, celebration doesn't have to be reserved for the big moments. Sometimes, the small wins are what matter most.

Let me tell you a story. When I was at my lowest, sitting in that Texas jail cell, there wasn't exactly a lot to celebrate. I'd lost everything—my freedom, my dignity, my son, my sense of who I was. But even in that dark place, I found tiny things to hold onto. Like the time I managed to get through a day without letting my anger take over. Or the time I made someone laugh during a conversation in the yard. Those moments didn't change my circumstances, but they reminded me that I still had some fight left in me. And that was worth celebrating.

The act of celebration is about more than just marking a moment—it's about reclaiming your joy. Life has a way of beating the joy out of us if we let it. Bills pile up, relationships get complicated, and the daily grind can make it feel like there's nothing to smile about. But when you celebrate, you're making a choice. You're saying, "F*ck you, stress. I'm still here, and I'm still finding reasons to smile." That's a powerful choice, one that can change how you see your life.

So how do you start celebrating every damn thing? First, change your definition of what's worth celebrating. Sure, promotions, milestones, and big wins are great. But what about the small, everyday victories? The ones that seem insignificant but add up over time? Like making it to the gym when you didn't feel like it. Or finally saying no to something you didn't want to do. Or resisting the urge to check your ex's Instagram for the fifth time that day. Those moments are worth celebrating because they're proof that you're showing up for yourself.

Second, make celebration a habit. Don't wait for someone else to throw you a party—be your own cheerleader. Maybe that means treating yourself to your favorite dessert after a long day. Maybe it's cranking up your favorite song and dancing around your living room like an idiot. Or maybe it's just taking a quiet moment to say, "Good job, me. I'm proud of you." The how doesn't matter as much as the why. The point is to acknowledge your wins and let yourself feel good about them.

Third, share your celebrations with others. Celebration is contagious, and when you share your joy, you invite others to do the same. Tell your friends about your small wins. Post that silly "I did the thing!" update on social media. Let the people who love you cheer you on, even if the moment feels small. Because the truth is, they're probably looking for reasons to celebrate, too. And your joy can inspire theirs.

Now, let's talk about the elephant in the room: guilt. So many of us feel guilty for celebrating ourselves, like we haven't "earned" it yet. F*ck that. You don't need anyone's permission to celebrate your life. You don't need to hit some arbitrary milestone or achieve some massive goal to feel proud of yourself. You're here, you're trying, and that's enough. Celebrate it.

Let me give you an example from my own life. When I finally started putting my story down on paper to write **I Won't Break**, I didn't wait until the book was finished to celebrate. I celebrated every chapter I completed, every late-night writing session I powered through, every time I found the courage to put my truth into words. Those small celebrations kept me going, even when self-doubt tried to convince me to quit. And when the book was finally done? That celebration felt even sweeter because I'd been honoring the journey all along.

Here's the bottom line: life isn't a highlight reel. It's a series of small, messy, beautiful moments strung together. And if you're waiting for the "big" moments to start celebrating, you're going to miss a lot of joy along the way. So, celebrate every damn thing. Celebrate the big wins, the small victories, and everything in between. Celebrate your progress, your resilience, and your ability to keep showing up, no matter how hard it gets.

Because the truth is, you're worth celebrating. Every damn day. So pop the champagne, light the candles, blast your favorite song—whatever makes you feel alive. You don't need a reason, and you sure as hell don't need permission. Celebrate because you can. Celebrate because you deserve it. And celebrate because, at the end of the day, life is too short not to.

CHAPTER TWENTY FIVE

Get Naked
(Metaphorically, Chill)

Alright, don't panic. I'm not telling you to strip down and start running through the streets in your birthday suit (unless that's your thing, no judgment). When I say "get naked," I'm talking about peeling back the layers of bullsh*t you've been wearing your whole life—the masks, the armor, the walls you've built to protect yourself from judgment, pain, or vulnerability. I'm talking about showing up as your raw, unfiltered, authentic self. Scars, flaws, and all.

Getting naked in this sense is about more than just being honest. It's about being real. And let's be honest, real is terrifying. Because when you're real, when you strip away all the bullsh*t, you're left with nothing to hide behind. It's just you—messy, imperfect, and vulnerable. But here's the thing: that's where the magic happens. That's where connection, growth, and freedom live. You can't truly love yourself—or let anyone else love you—until you're willing to get naked.

Now, I get it. Getting metaphorically naked is f*cking hard. Most of us have spent years building up layers to protect ourselves. Maybe it started in childhood, when someone made fun of you for being too sensitive, so you decided to toughen up. Or maybe it came later, after heartbreaks and betrayals taught you that vulnerability equals pain. Whatever the reason, those layers served a purpose. They kept you safe—or at least, they made you feel safe. But now? They're keeping you stuck.

I've worn plenty of layers in my life. Growing up in the foster care system, I learned early on that being vulnerable was dangerous. I built walls so high, even I couldn't see over them. I pretended to be fine when I wasn't. I tried to be strong when I felt like falling apart. And for a long time, I thought that was the only way to survive. But here's what I've learned: survival isn't living. And you can't truly live if you're too scared to be seen.

The moment I started to get naked was the moment my life began to change. It wasn't one big epiphany—it was a series of small, terrifying choices. Like the first time I told my story to someone I trusted, knowing they could judge me but hoping they wouldn't. Or the first time I admitted to myself that I needed help instead of trying to tough it out on my own. Each time I let down my guard, it felt like I was risking everything. But each time, I discovered something incredible: the world didn't end. In fact, my world got bigger. My connections got deeper. And I started to feel something I hadn't felt in a long time: free.

So, how do you start getting naked (again, metaphorically)? First, take an honest inventory of the layers you're wearing. What are you hiding behind? Is it the mask of perfection? The tough-guy act? The "I'm fine" facade? Identify your layers, and ask yourself why they're there. What purpose are they serving? And more importantly, are they still serving you?

Second, start small. Getting naked doesn't mean you have to spill your deepest secrets to a stranger on the subway. It can be as simple as admitting to a friend that you're struggling, saying no when you mean it, or letting someone see a part of you that you've been hiding. Vulnerability is a muscle, and the more you use it, the stronger it gets.

Third, surround yourself with people who make you feel safe. Not everyone deserves to see you naked (metaphorically or otherwise). Choose the ones who've earned your trust—the ones who don't judge you for your scars but celebrate them as proof of your resilience. For me, that person was Anthony. He saw me at my lowest, when I felt like nothing but a collection of mistakes, and he loved me anyway. That kind of unconditional acceptance? It's life-changing.

And finally, give yourself grace. Getting naked is a process, not a one-time event. You're going to have moments where you want to put the layers back on, where vulnerability feels too hard and too risky. That's okay. The important thing is to keep trying. Each time you let yourself be seen, you take one step closer to living fully and authentically.

Let me share one of the most vulnerable moments of my life. Writing **I Won't Break** was like standing naked in front of the world. Every chapter, every story, every raw truth I put on the page felt like ripping off a layer of armor I'd been wearing for years. I was terrified that people would judge me, that they'd see my flaws and think less of me. But you know what happened? People connected with my story. They saw themselves in my struggles, my mistakes, and my resilience. And that connection? That was worth every moment of fear.

Here's the truth: getting naked is scary. But staying covered up is exhausting. It's lonely. And it's no way to live. When you let yourself be seen, you create space for real connection, real growth, and real freedom. You give yourself permission to stop pretending, to stop performing, and to just be.

So, peel back the layers. Show up as you are. Get naked—not because it's easy, but because it's worth it. Because the world doesn't need another polished, filtered, perfect facade. It needs you—raw, real, and unapologetically you. And trust me, once you start living that way, you'll never want to go back.

Part Six: Burnout, Boundaries, and Balance

Let's talk about burnout—the silent, soul-sucking beast that creeps up on you when you're too busy trying to be everything for everyone. You know the feeling: you're running on fumes, your to-do list is longer than a CVS receipt, and even the idea of rest makes you feel guilty. Sound familiar? Yeah, that's burnout. And it doesn't just hit you like a brick—it grinds you down slowly, stealing your joy, your energy, and your sense of self. But here's the good news: burnout isn't the end of the road. It's your wake-up call.

In this part of the book, we're going to tackle the big three: burnout, boundaries, and balance. Why? Because these three things are like the holy trinity of survival in a world that never stops demanding more from you. Burnout is the result of giving too much of yourself without replenishing your energy. Boundaries are what protect your peace and give you the space to breathe. And balance? That's the elusive middle ground where you stop living in extremes and start thriving instead of just surviving.

This isn't about finding some perfect "work-life balance" (spoiler: it doesn't exist). It's about getting real with yourself about what you need, what you want, and what you're no longer willing to tolerate. It's about saying no to the sh*t that drains you and yes to the things that bring you joy. It's about learning that rest isn't a luxury—it's a necessity. And it's about reclaiming your time, your energy, and your life.

In this section, we'll dive deep into the signs of burnout and how to recover from it without throwing your life into chaos. We'll explore the art of setting boundaries that actually stick (without feeling like an a**hole), and we'll talk about how to build a life that feels balanced, even when everything around you is screaming for your attention. Because here's the truth: you can't pour from an empty cup. And if you're going to live your best, boldest life, you've got to take care of yourself first.

So, if you're tired of running on empty, if you're ready to stop being everything for everyone, and if you're craving a life that actually feels good to live, this part is for you. Let's get into it. It's time to reclaim your time, your energy, and your damn sanity.

CHAPTER TWENTY SIX

Burnout Is Bullsh*t

Burnout is a sneaky little bastard. It doesn't come crashing in like some big, dramatic breakdown—it creeps in slowly, taking little pieces of you until you're running on fumes and wondering why you're so damn tired all the time. And here's the kicker: burnout isn't just about being overworked. It's about being over-given, over-stressed, and over your own boundaries. It's about pouring everything you have into everyone else until there's nothing left for you. And let me tell you: that sh*t is unsustainable.

Let's call burnout what it really is: a thief. It robs you of your energy, your passion, and your joy. It takes something you used to love—your work, your relationships, even your hobbies—and turns it into a source of stress and resentment. Suddenly, everything feels like a chore, and the simplest tasks drain you more than they should. But here's the thing: burnout isn't a personal failing. It's not about you being weak or lazy or "not tough enough." Burnout happens because you've been conditioned to believe that your worth is tied to how much you can produce, how much you can give, and how much you can endure.

I've been there. I've burned out so many times, I should've earned a loyalty card. When I was at the height of my psychic career, I was working nonstop, trying to be everything to everyone. I wanted to help people, sure, but I was also chasing validation. I thought that if I could just do enough, achieve enough, and give enough, I'd finally feel worthy. But instead of feeling fulfilled, I felt empty. Exhausted. Resentful. And the worst part? I didn't know how to stop. I was so deep in the cycle of burnout that the idea of slowing down felt like failure.

Here's the hard truth: burnout doesn't just happen. It's not some random act of God. It's the result of ignoring your needs, your limits, and your boundaries for too long. It's what happens when you keep saying "yes" to sh*t you should've said "no" to. When you put everyone else's needs ahead of your own. When you treat rest like a reward instead of a basic human necessity. Burnout isn't inevitable—it's preventable. But only if you're willing to do the work to protect your energy.

So, how do you stop burnout in its tracks? First, you've got to recognize the signs. Burnout isn't just physical exhaustion—it's emotional and mental exhaustion, too. It's the feeling of dread you get when you think about your to-do list. It's snapping at people over small things because your patience is shot. It's losing interest in things you used to love because you're too drained to care. If any of this sounds familiar, it's time to take a hard look at how you've been living.

Second, you've got to start saying "no." And I mean really saying it—not the half-assed, "Maybe later" or "Let me think about it" that eventually turns into a reluctant yes. Saying no is a skill, and like any skill, it takes practice. Start small. Say no to the meeting that could've been an email. Say no to the favor that you don't have the bandwidth for. Say no to the toxic friend who only calls when they need something. Every no is a step toward reclaiming your energy.

Third, prioritize rest like your life depends on it—because it does. Rest isn't just about sleeping (although let's be honest, you probably need more of that, too). Rest is about giving yourself permission to pause, recharge, and do nothing without guilt. It's about listening to your body and your mind when they're begging you to slow down. And it's about understanding that rest isn't a sign of weakness—it's a sign of wisdom.

Finally, let go of the bullsh*t idea that you have to do it all. Newsflash: you don't. The world won't end if you take a day off. Your worth isn't tied to your productivity. And anyone who expects you to be everything, all the time, for everyone, isn't someone you need in your life. Burnout thrives on the lie that you're not enough unless you're constantly doing more. But the truth? You're enough just as you are, even when you're doing nothing at all.

Let me tell you about the moment I finally called bullsh*t on burnout. It was after Caleb was taken from me. I'd spent years trying to hold everything together, pretending I was fine, and pushing through the pain. But one day, I hit a wall. I couldn't keep going. And in that moment, I realized something: burnout wasn't noble. It wasn't a badge of honor. It was a wake-up call. It was my body and mind screaming at me to stop, to breathe, to take care of myself for once. And when I finally listened? That's when the healing began.

So, if you're feeling burned out right now, hear me loud and clear: burnout is bullsh*t. It's not a badge of honor, and it's not something you have to live with. You have the power to stop the cycle, set boundaries, and reclaim your energy. It won't be easy, and it won't happen overnight, but it's worth it. Because you're worth it.

Remember, you can't pour from an empty cup. So stop running on fumes, stop ignoring your needs, and start putting yourself first. The world can wait. Your well-being can't. Burnout is bullsh*t—so let's leave it behind and start living instead.

CHAPTER TWENTY SEVEN

Build Boundaries, Burn Bridges (When Needed)

Let's get something straight—boundaries are not just polite "lines" you put up to keep people from crossing into your personal space. Boundaries are survival tools. They are the lines in the sand that say, "This is where I end and you begin." They're the walls you build to protect your time, your energy, and your peace of mind. And here's the thing: most of us suck at setting boundaries. We're taught from a young age to be "nice," to always accommodate others, to put other people's needs ahead of our own. But here's the brutal truth: **being nice** is a one-way ticket to burnout, resentment, and feeling like you're being used by the world.

Now, I get it. Setting boundaries can feel uncomfortable, especially if you've spent your life being the "good one"—the one who doesn't say no, who always puts others first. But let me tell you something: **you cannot pour from an empty cup.** You can't give what you don't have. And if you're running on fumes trying to please everyone around you, eventually you're going to break. I don't care how tough you are, how much you can handle, or how many hours you've worked without a break. Everyone has a breaking point, and the sooner you realize that your boundaries are the foundation of your sanity, the better.

The first thing you've got to do is **get crystal clear on what your boundaries actually are.** What do you need to feel good? What can you give without feeling drained? What's a hard no? And what's a "don't even think about it" no? You can't set boundaries if you don't know where you stand, so spend some time really digging into your own needs. It's not selfish, it's survival. And trust me, **if you don't know where you draw the line, other people will keep drawing it for you.** They'll keep demanding more from you, taking what they can get, and you'll be left wondering why you feel empty.

Let's take work, for example. How many times have you been asked to take on more than you should? To stay late for something that doesn't even concern you? To sacrifice your personal time because "it's just one more thing"? **Stop that sh*t.** If you're always saying yes, you're teaching people that your time is expendable. **Your time is not expendable**—it's precious. And if you don't set a clear boundary with your work, they will run you into the ground, and then move on to the next person. Remember this: your job is not your life. It's a means to an end. Your health, happiness, and relationships are where the real value is.

The second thing to understand is that **not all relationships are worth saving.** Yep, I said it. Boundaries aren't just about keeping the good in; they're also about **cutting the toxic out.** You know who I'm talking about—those people who drain the life out of you, who don't respect your time, who suck up all your energy without giving anything in return. These are the people who will ask for your time, energy, and emotional support, but won't give you a damn thing back. And here's the reality check: **you don't owe these people anything.** There is no law that says you have to keep toxic people in your life. If someone is constantly disrespecting your boundaries, **burn that bridge.** You don't have to set fire to the relationship with anger or drama (unless that's your thing, no judgment), but you do need to make a decision: **this person is no longer a part of my life.**

And that, my friend, is called "burning bridges." But here's the thing—you're not burning it because you're mad or petty. You're burning it because **you have the right to protect yourself.** The people who love and respect you will understand your boundaries. The people who don't—well, they can take a walk. And that's where the bridge-burning comes in. It's not about being vindictive, it's about cutting your losses and moving on. The people who don't get it? They're not meant to be in your future.

Now, don't get me wrong. **Burning bridges is not about being reckless** or going scorched earth on everyone who rubs you the wrong way. But when you've tried to communicate your boundaries, when you've given second chances, and when you've still been disrespected or used, it's time to take action. **You don't need permission to protect your peace.** You don't need to keep people around who don't add to your life or respect your limits. That's not cold, that's smart.

And yes, I've been there. I've had to cut off people who were once family. People who used to be my friends. And I'll be honest with you—it wasn't easy. At first, I felt guilty. I questioned myself. I thought, "Am I being too harsh?" But then I realized: I wasn't being harsh. I was being real with myself. And when I let go of the relationships that were holding me back, I made space for the ones that really mattered. The ones that brought me peace, support, and love. The ones that respected my time and energy.

It's a powerful thing to finally realize that you don't need to explain your boundaries to anyone. You don't need to justify why you need space, why you need to say no, or why you're stepping away from a relationship that no longer serves you. You've got to take back your power, and that starts by setting clear, non-negotiable boundaries with the world around you. You'll be amazed at how much peace and freedom comes when you stop apologizing for taking care of yourself.

But hey, if you're still not convinced, let me ask you this: If you don't protect your boundaries, **who will?** If you don't stand up for your time, your needs, and your peace, **who will?** You can't expect people to respect something you're not willing to defend. So stop bending over backward trying to please people who wouldn't do the same for you. Build your boundaries. Burn your bridges. And let go of the things, the people, and the situations that are dragging you down.

You deserve peace. You deserve respect. And you deserve to live a life that's yours to control. So go ahead—**burn those bridges when you need to.** Keep the ones that are worth crossing. The rest? Let them burn.

CHAPTER TWENTY EIGHT

Self-Care Ain't Selfish

Let's get one thing straight right now: **self-care is not selfish.** It's not a luxury, it's not indulgence, and it sure as hell isn't something you should feel guilty about. Too many people get this twisted. We've been conditioned to think that taking care of ourselves, putting ourselves first, and setting time aside for our own well-being is some kind of "optional extra" in life. Like we're supposed to spend all our time serving others, burning ourselves out, and never asking for anything in return. **Well, f*ck that.** You're not a martyr, and you're not a machine. You're a human being, and you deserve to take care of yourself, just like anyone else.

The problem is that society has this sick habit of making us feel like we're not allowed to prioritize ourselves. From an early age, we're taught to "be there" for everyone else. Whether it's our parents, our friends, or the world in general, there's this unwritten rule that we have to always give, always serve, always put everyone's needs ahead of our own. And while that sounds noble in theory, the reality is it's a recipe for exhaustion, burnout, and resentment.

You can't be a good partner, friend, parent, or even employee if you're running on empty. **You can't give what you don't have.** If you're constantly depleting your energy for others, you're not going to have anything left to show up as the best version of yourself. And guess what? That's not helping anyone. It's actually doing more harm than good. People around you will notice when you're drained, when you're overwhelmed, when you're trying to keep everything together but barely holding on. **You're no good to anyone if you're falling apart inside.**

So what does self-care really look like? Is it just about taking bubble baths and lighting candles? Sure, if that works for you. But it's much more than that. **Self-care is about setting boundaries**—saying no when you need to, cutting out the toxic people who suck the life out of you, and making sure you have time to recharge. It's about taking your mental and emotional health seriously. If you're feeling like crap, you don't have to push through like a robot. Take the day off. Say no to plans. Cancel that dinner date if you're not feeling up to it. **It's okay to put yourself first.**

Self-care also means tending to your physical health. We've all heard the saying, "If you don't have your health, you don't have anything." It's the truth. And I know it's easy to push this to the back burner when life's busy, but the body you've got is the only one you're going to get, and it's your job to take care of it. You don't need to be at the gym 5 days a week or follow some crazy diet plan. Just make sure you're moving, eating well, and getting enough sleep. Don't use "work" or "stress" as excuses to ignore your body. If you're constantly tired, aching, or mentally drained, it's because you're not giving your body what it needs. And if you're running on fumes, everything else in your life will suffer.

Mental health is self-care, too. Taking time to de-stress, meditate, or even talk to a therapist is just as important as getting enough sleep. If you're mentally burned out, if your anxiety is through the roof, if you're feeling depressed, it's time to do something about it. **It's time to treat your mind like the precious tool it is.** And let's be real—taking care of your mental health is often the hardest part because it requires vulnerability and honesty. It requires you to confront the sh*t *you've been ignoring, whether that's trauma, stress, or feelings of inadequacy. But facing that sh*t* head-on is how you heal, and you **cannot** ignore your mental health forever. **You deserve to feel good in your mind and your body.**

So, why do we still feel guilty about self-care? Why do we still think it's indulgent or selfish? I'll tell you why—it's because we've been conditioned to believe that our worth comes from what we give to others. But here's the kicker: **your worth is not based on how much you do for others, it's based on who you are.** And who you are deserves love, respect, and care. If you're running on empty, you're not going to show up for the people who need you. You're not going to be the best partner, parent, friend, or employee that you can be. You'll just be a shell of yourself.

Let me tell you something: **you're not obligated to burn yourself out for anyone.** It's okay to step back, take a break, and say, "I need to put myself first right now." It's okay to not answer every call, reply to every text, or go to every single event. It's okay to cancel plans when you're feeling overwhelmed. You don't owe anyone an explanation. Your well-being is not up for debate.

And you know what? **You'll be amazed at how much better you feel when you stop apologizing for taking care of yourself.** You'll feel more energized, more grounded, and more connected to your own needs. You'll start showing up as the best version of yourself—not because you're trying to please everyone, but because you're finally taking care of your own damn needs. And when you do that, everyone around you will benefit. You'll have more to give. You'll be more present. And you'll feel better about who you are.

Self-care isn't selfish. It's self-preservation. And if you're not taking care of yourself, you're not doing anyone any favors. So, take the time. Put your needs first. And remember that it's not only okay to care for yourself, it's absolutely necessary.

CHAPTER TWENTY NINE

Find Your Freaking Joy

Listen, I don't care how much life has thrown at you, how many times you've been knocked down, or how many people have told you to suck it up and "be grateful" for what you have. **You deserve to find your joy,** and you need to start doing it now. Right now. No more waiting for the perfect moment, no more holding off until the stars align, or until your bank account looks just right. **Your joy is not on hold—it's already available to you.** You just have to look for it.

So, here's the thing: we live in a world that constantly tells us we need more to be happy. You need more money. You need a better job. You need a partner who's better looking, smarter, and more successful than the last one. You need to lose those last 10 pounds. You need to buy that shiny new thing. There's this constant, relentless pressure to always want more, be more, and do more. And guess what? It's a load of crap. **That sh*t does not equal joy.** If you're waiting for all the stars to align before you allow yourself to be happy, you'll be waiting forever.

Joy is not found in the things you have or the things you don't have. It's not something that's out of reach, dangling on the horizon like a carrot you'll never catch. Joy is something that you *choose.* Every single damn day. It's about waking up and choosing to find the good in the day, even if the world around you is a complete dumpster fire. It's about choosing to be present, choosing to laugh at the chaos, choosing to see the beauty in the small things that are easy to overlook. You can choose joy, no matter how messy, how broken, or how difficult things get. **Joy is not earned, it's cultivated.**

This is the part where a lot of people f*ck up. They think that joy is something that's earned by meeting some checklist of "success" or "achievement." They're looking for joy in the wrong places, waiting for their lives to be "perfect" before they can enjoy anything. But let me tell you: **joy does not care about your achievements.** It doesn't care about how much you've accomplished or how many Instagram followers you have. It doesn't care about your job title, your bank account, or your relationship status. Joy is about being able to sit with yourself and find peace in the present moment—**and that's the secret most people never figure out.**

You have to stop waiting for life to give you a damn break. Life is never going to be perfect. **There is no "perfect time" to experience joy,** and if you keep waiting for it, you're going to miss the whole point. Life is messy, unpredictable, and chaotic, and that's where the magic happens. When you learn to find joy in the mess, in the imperfection, in the chaos—that's when you unlock the kind of happiness that sticks. You don't have to have your sh*t together to find joy. You don't need the perfect body, the perfect relationship, or the perfect career. What you need is to let go of the idea that you're not worthy of joy until you've "achieved" something. **That's the trap.** It's all about embracing the imperfect, messy, beautifully chaotic life that's happening right now.

And here's the kicker: the more you practice finding joy in the little things, the more it starts to show up. It's like a muscle. At first, it's hard to find anything to be joyful about. It feels fake, forced, like you're pretending. But if you keep looking, if you keep searching for it in unexpected places, joy will start to reveal itself in the most surprising ways. You'll start noticing the small wins—the little victories in your day-today life. Maybe it's getting through the day without a meltdown. Maybe it's having a cup of coffee with a friend who makes you laugh. Maybe it's the first moment of peace you've had in days. **Those small moments are joy, too.** They all add up. And the more you focus on them, the more joy you'll find.

Finding joy is about embracing your freakin' self. It's about recognizing that you are worthy of happiness, no matter what anyone else says or how messed up your life might feel right now. **Your life does not need to be "fixed" before you can experience joy.** You don't need to have everything figured out. In fact, your joy doesn't depend on being "fixed" at all. It's about finding freedom in the chaos, letting go of the need to control everything, and allowing yourself to be exactly who you are, flaws and all.

So, what does this look like in practice? It's simple: **find the things that light you up.** The things that make you smile. The things that make you feel alive. It could be spending time with people who make you laugh until your stomach hurts. It could be working on a passion project that lights you on fire, or getting lost in a hobby that makes you forget about the world. Maybe it's going for a walk in nature, dancing like no one's watching, or sitting quietly with your thoughts and just breathing. The point is, **find the things that make your soul smile and let them fill you up.**

When you learn to find your freakin' joy, you stop giving a sh*t *about what anyone else thinks. You stop comparing yourself to others. You stop looking for external validation, because you know that your joy comes from within. You are the creator of your own happiness. It's all on you. The world might throw all kinds of sh*t your way, but if you choose joy, if you choose to see the good in the chaos, you'll become unstoppable.*

And remember this: **joy is not a destination, it's a way of living.** It's not something that's waiting for you at the finish line. It's something you can have in the mess, in the struggle, in the hard times. **So stop waiting for the perfect moment.** The perfect moment is now. And if you're looking for joy, stop searching for it in the wrong places. Start searching for it in the small, everyday moments that make life worth living. That's where the magic is. And that's where you'll find your joy.

CHAPTER THIRTY

Simplify Your F*cking Life

Alright, it's time to get real. You've got a lot of sh*t going on in your life, right? We all do. We're juggling jobs, relationships, family drama, bills, health problems, personal goals, and all the other messes that life throws at us. But here's the thing—you don't need to be overwhelmed by it all. You **don't** need to keep adding more stuff to your already crowded plate. **You don't need to be so damn busy all the time.** In fact, simplifying your life could be the best thing you can do for your mental health, happiness, and sanity.

Stop trying to do everything. **Stop trying to be everything to everyone.** That's a one-way ticket to burnout and resentment. If your life feels like a never-ending to-do list, full of obligations and expectations that drain you, you've got to hit the reset button. **You don't have to do it all.** You really don't. And anyone who tells you that you do can go take a long walk off a short pier.

The truth is, you're probably caught up in this cycle of over-committing because you've been taught that busy equals successful. That if you're not constantly hustling, you're failing. Well, here's a big f*cking secret: **busyness does not equal success.** In fact, it might be the reason you feel like you're constantly running in circles and never getting anywhere. **Simplifying your life is the real success.**

Start by identifying what's actually important. And by that, I mean, what do you *really* care about? What's worth your energy and time? And most importantly—**what isn't?** Look, I know we all have responsibilities, and I'm not saying you can just throw everything out the window and live like a monk. But there are so many things in your life right now that are sucking up your time, your energy, and your f*cking happiness for no good reason. **Get rid of those things.**

Maybe you've been holding onto toxic relationships because you feel obligated, or maybe you've been saying yes to things you really don't give a sh*t about just to please other people. Maybe you've got a bunch of material possessions that you don't even need, but they're just cluttering up your space and your mind. Well, guess what? It's time to **simplify.** It's time to get rid of the things, the people, and the situations that drain you.

I'm not saying go full minimalist and start tossing out everything in your house. But I am saying that **the more stuff you have—physically, mentally, and emotionally—the more complicated your life becomes.** The more you carry, the more you're going to feel like you're drowning. So start paring things down. Start saying no. Start focusing on the stuff that makes you feel alive, that brings you peace, and that genuinely adds value to your life.

Simplifying your life also means **getting clear on your boundaries.** Stop letting people walk all over you. Stop letting your time be consumed by things that don't serve you. Start protecting your energy like it's the most valuable thing you've got (because it is). And here's the kicker—**you don't need to justify your boundaries.** If something or someone is taking more from you than it's giving, that sh*t has to go.

And while you're at it, **stop overcomplicating your own mind.** We've all been there: you lay awake at night, stressing about everything that could go wrong, obsessing over every little detail, second-guessing every decision. But here's a little secret—**most of that crap you're worrying about never even happens.** Your mind has a way of blowing things out of proportion. It gets caught in cycles of "what if" scenarios and fears of failure. And you know what? It's all a waste of energy. **Simplify your thinking.** Take things one step at a time. Focus on the present moment. The rest? It'll work itself out. Or, it won't. But either way, **you can't control every little thing.**

In the end, simplifying your life is about stripping away the unnecessary noise and focusing on what truly matters. It's about giving yourself permission to stop hustling for approval, stop running on empty, and stop making everything harder than it needs to be.

So, here's the deal: **stop overcomplicating everything**—your relationships, your work, your self-worth, your damn schedule. Keep it simple. Focus on what's important. Get rid of the toxic sh*t. Protect your peace. And let go of the need to prove something to anyone. Because the truth is, **you've already done enough.** You're worthy of peace, of rest, and of joy.

Let's make it easy. Let's make it simple. Because life doesn't need to be this f*cking hard.

Part Seven: Resilience is Sexy

Alright, buckle up, because this is where we turn up the heat. Resilience—yeah, you heard me right—is sexy. You're probably thinking, "Wait, what? Sexy? Are we talking about abs or a nice jawline here?" Nah, fam. **I'm talking about the kind of sexy that comes from within.** The kind that's earned, not bought. The kind that gets stronger the more life tries to kick your ass. It's the kind of sexy that says, "I've been through hell and back, and I'm still standing, looking better than ever."

We're living in a world where everyone's obsessed with perfection—filtered photos, fake smiles, and showing off all the good stuff while hiding the struggles. But let's be honest, **real resilience? That's the ultimate turn-on.** Because resilience doesn't give up when the going gets tough. Resilience doesn't break when the world piles on the pressure. Resilience keeps fighting, keeps growing, and refuses to stay down—even when life tries to knock you out.

You know what's more attractive than a pretty face or a perfect body? **The ability to rise after falling, again and again.** It's in those moments when you've been tested, pushed to your limits, and still found a way to bounce back. It's the strength to get back up, even when you're covered in scars, bruises, and a whole lot of sweat. It's that **"I won't quit" attitude** that makes people sit up, take notice, and respect you.

In this part of the book, we're diving into what it really means to be resilient. Not the "I'm fine" kind of resilient. **Nope.** The real kind. The kind that doesn't ignore pain but uses it as fuel. The kind that doesn't just bounce back, but **bounces forward.** Because let's face it: if you can handle the sh*t life throws at you, you become a force of nature. People start to notice that, and trust me, they can't look away.

So, let's talk about how to be resilient as hell, even when everything is falling apart. Let's break down the walls that try to keep you small, and build up the fire inside that makes you unapologetically strong. Get ready, because **this part is where we turn that inner fire into something unstoppable.**

Resilience is sexy, my friend, and by the end of this section, you'll know exactly how to turn that power into your secret weapon. And trust me, it's going to make you *irresistible*.

CHAPTER THIRTY ONE

Scars Are Sexy

Let's talk about scars. Not the kind that come from a reckless childhood or a drunken night out (though those can be fun stories, too). I'm talking about the real scars—the ones that tell the story of your survival. The ones that are etched into your soul, your heart, and sometimes even your mind, because life has a way of leaving a mark, whether we want it to or not.

We all have scars. They come in all shapes, sizes, and forms. Some are obvious—maybe you've got physical scars that you can trace with your fingers like battle wounds from some war you didn't ask to fight. Others are hidden, invisible to the naked eye, but they sting just the same. The emotional scars. The scars of abandonment, betrayal, loss, or shame. The scars that make us question our worth and wonder if we'll ever be whole again.

Here's the thing I want you to remember, though: **scars are sexy.**

Wait, what? Sexy? Are you serious?

Yeah, I am. Let me explain. **Scars represent strength.** They're the proof that you didn't give up, even when the world tried to crush you. They're your badge of honor. Your resilience. Every scar you have is a story of survival, and that story makes you who you are. You're not perfect—no one is—but those scars, the way they shape you and show the world what you've been through, are what make you real. And **real is f*cking sexy**.

Let's get real for a second. We're constantly told we need to hide our flaws. Society bombards us with the idea that we have to be perfect—physically, mentally, emotionally. Social media's a damn highlight reel of flawless lives, edited photos, and perfectly curated images. We see that sh*t and think, "I'm not enough," but that's a lie. **Perfection is overrated.** It's the cracks and the imperfections that make us unique, and it's those very scars that make us stand out in the world.

Think about the people you admire, the ones who truly stand out. Are they the ones who've sailed through life without a scratch, without a bruise? Hell no. It's the ones who've been through the toughest sh*t and came out stronger. They wear their scars like a badge of honor because they know something the rest of the world doesn't: **scars don't define you—they refine you.** They shape you into a more powerful, authentic, and resilient version of yourself.

Those scars? They're evidence that you kept going when life tried to break you. **You didn't stay down.** And that, my friend, is what makes you sexy as hell. It's that quiet strength, that inner fire that shines through no matter how many times you've been knocked down.

It's easy to hide from your scars, to be ashamed of them, or to pretend they're not there. But why the hell would you do that? **Show them off.** Wear them like the *fcking battle scars they are. Wear them with pride, because they tell a story that's yours and yours alone. They say, "I survived. I made it through the hard sh*t. And I'm still here."*

And if you think no one notices? Trust me, they do. People are drawn to strength. They're drawn to authenticity. And when they see you wearing your scars with confidence, they can't help but admire you.

So stop hiding. Stop pretending. Stop being ashamed of what you've been through. **Your scars are sexy.** They're part of who you are, and who you are is powerful, beautiful, and unapologetically real. And if someone can't see that, well, they don't deserve to be in your life anyway.

Embrace your scars. Embrace the sh*t *that's been thrown at you. Own every single mark that's been left on you, because they're not weaknesses—they're **fcking power**. The next time you look in the mirror, instead of covering up your scars, give them a nod of respect. Because they're the reason you're as strong as you are. And that, my friend, is sexy as hell.*

CHAPTER THIRTY TWO

F*ck Fear

Fear. It's that little voice inside your head that tells you all the reasons you *can't* do something. It's the grip that tightens around your chest, making your heart race, your palms sweat, and your stomach drop when you even think about stepping out of your comfort zone. Fear has a way of creeping into your mind and paralyzing you, convincing you that you're not good enough, that you're not ready, that you'll fail—and fail spectacularly.

But you know what? **F*ck fear.**

Seriously. F*ck it right in its self-doubting, paralyzing, limiting little face.

Fear is nothing but a liar, a thief, and the ultimate cockblock when it comes to living your best life. It's the thing that keeps you stuck in the same place, replaying the same old story, day in and day out. It's the reason you don't start that business, ask for that raise, or speak your truth. It's the reason you stay in toxic relationships, continue to live beneath your potential, and sell yourself short.

And here's the kicker—**fear is *always* with you.** It never leaves. The only thing that changes is how you deal with it.

The difference between the people who live their lives on their own terms and the people who are held back by fear isn't that one group is fearless—they just know how to keep going **in spite of fear.** Fear doesn't disappear. But you know what you can do? You can flip it the bird and say, "I'm doing this anyway."

Let me break it down: fear is the voice that tells you *not to try*—so you try anyway. Fear is the thing that says *you'll fail*, but failure is just a stepping stone to success, not the end of the road. Fear says, *what if it goes wrong?* But here's the reality: **what if it goes right?** What if you take the leap and discover something amazing on the other side? What if you succeed beyond your wildest dreams?

Fear holds you back by controlling the narrative, playing on your insecurities, and showing you all the worst-case scenarios. But **fuck the worst-case scenarios.** The truth is, most of the shit we fear never even happens. We spend all this time worrying about things that, more often than not, are out of our control or don't come to fruition. We're essentially living in a future that *hasn't even happened yet*, and allowing it to rob us of the present.

So, how do you stop fear from running the show?

You don't give it the power. You acknowledge it—yeah, it's there, it's part of you—but you don't let it control your actions. You look fear in the face and say, "I see you, but I'm not afraid of you. In fact, I'm going to do the thing that scares me the most, because that's where the magic happens."

The thing about fear is that it doesn't give a f*ck about your potential. It doesn't care if you're meant for more. It's only job is to stop you. It feeds on your doubt and thrives on your hesitation. But here's the truth—**fear only wins if you let it.**

Fear is a skill you need to learn to master, just like anything else in life. The more you push through it, the more you realize it's all smoke and mirrors. That voice in your head? It doesn't have to be the final say. That tightness in your chest? That's just your body reacting to something new, and guess what? It's okay to feel uncomfortable.

So let's stop letting fear make decisions for us. Let's stop making *choices* based on avoiding discomfort. Take risks. Get uncomfortable. Fail a few times. But do it anyway, because on the other side of fear is **growth.** There's freedom. There's success. There's living a life you can be proud of.

In fact, you're going to look at fear as a sign that you're on the right path. When you feel fear creeping in, you'll smile and say, "Alright, this is it. Time to do the thing that scares the hell out of me."

Because that's the only way you're ever going to get ahead. And if you want to live the life you truly deserve, you have to stop asking for permission and start telling fear to get the f*ck out of the way.

So, here's the final word on fear: **F*ck it.** Fear is the enemy of progress, and if you want to thrive, you can't afford to let it dictate your life. Take that leap. Do the thing that scares you. And when you land on the other side, you'll realize it was worth every moment of terror. Because in the end, the most satisfying thing is not being fearless—it's *being brave* enough to face fear and do it anyway.

Fear doesn't own you. **You own it.** Now go take what's yours.

CHAPTER THIRTY THREE

Life Is Gonna Hurt. Keep Going Anyway

Welcome to reality. Here's the harsh truth: **life is going to hurt**. Like, a lot. The kind of hurt that's deep and unexpected, the kind that leaves scars, bruises, and a whole lot of questions. Whether it's the pain of losing someone you love, the sting of betrayal, or the weight of your own mistakes, life will hand you some shit you don't deserve. It will knock you down, it will make you question everything, and it will make you feel like you're never going to get up again.

But here's the thing—**you have to keep going anyway**.

It's easy to get stuck in the pain. It's easy to wallow, to retreat, to hide from the world and hope that it all just goes away. And, hell, maybe sometimes it feels like the only thing you *want* to do is curl up into a ball and give up. Life will give you plenty of reasons to throw in the towel, pack it in, and call it quits. I'm not here to sugarcoat shit. But if you take the easy way out, if you let that hurt define you, then you've already lost. And that's not what I'm about.

The thing is, hurt doesn't have to be the end of your story—it can be the beginning of something stronger. The pain, the heartache, the failures—all of it can be a catalyst for growth. But only if you keep going. The world doesn't stop just because you're hurting. Life doesn't pause for you to catch your breath. And I'm not saying you need to be a robot, pushing through without feeling anything. It's okay to feel pain, it's okay to grieve, it's okay to hurt like hell. But after that moment of pain, **you have to choose to keep going.**

And you know what? That's the hardest part. It's easy to quit. It's easy to throw your hands up and say, "I'm done." But what's the alternative? Staying stuck in the hurt forever? Sitting in that same dark room, replaying the same sad story over and over? That's not living. That's existing, and even then, it's not really existing. It's stagnating.

To truly live, you have to embrace the pain and keep moving forward anyway.

I'm not saying it won't be hard. Hell, it will be. You're going to face times when everything feels like it's falling apart, when the world feels like it's crumbling around you, and when you feel like you're running on empty. And there's no getting around that—it's part of the deal. Life isn't going to pamper you. It's not going to be fair. It's going to throw punches, and some of them are going to hurt like a motherfucker. But here's the catch—**you can take the punch and get back up.** Because getting knocked down doesn't mean you have to stay there. Getting hurt doesn't mean you have to stop.

You are going to face loss. You are going to face rejection. You are going to face the consequences of your own choices and, sometimes, the consequences of other people's mistakes. And it's going to feel like everything you've worked for has crumbled. It's going to feel like you're too broken to pick up the pieces. But let me tell you, you're not broken—**you're human**. And as much as life hurts, you are also capable of withstanding it. You have survived every single moment that's brought you here. You've lived through every ounce of pain you've felt so far, and you're still standing. That's something to be proud of.

So, when life hurts—and it will—when you feel like you've hit rock bottom, when you're gasping for air, and when you feel like you're drowning in the weight of it all—**keep going anyway.** Do it for yourself. Do it because you know you're stronger than the pain. Do it because you have something to prove—not to anyone else, but to yourself.

Life is never going to be perfect. It's not going to hand you a fairy tale. And that's a damn good thing, because perfection is boring as hell anyway. It's the messy, painful, real parts that shape you, that build you into who you are supposed to be. It's in the struggle that we find our strength. It's in the setbacks that we learn resilience. And it's in the hurt that we discover what we're truly capable of.

When life throws a punch, don't just stand there and take it—**punch back.** Keep going, even when it feels like you can't. Keep going when you think there's nothing left. Because I promise you, there's always more to you than you think. You've survived up until now, and you'll survive what's coming next. That's the power you have—**the power to keep going no matter how much it hurts.**

And remember, the best part about pain is that it always ends. It may not feel like it, but it does. Time keeps moving, and things do get better. Maybe not in the way you expect, and maybe not when you want it to, but they do get better. And when they do, you'll realize that every bit of hurt was worth it. Because it led you to this moment—the moment when you kept going anyway.

So, take a deep breath. Push through the pain. And keep f*cking going.

CHAPTER THIRTY FOUR

Rebuild Stronger

There's this idea that when you're broken, you stay broken forever. That once you've been shattered, it's all over. Well, let me be the first to tell you—**that's a load of crap**.

Being broken isn't the end of the road, it's the beginning of a new one. When life knocks you down and you feel like you've hit rock bottom, the world's not telling you that you're done—it's giving you an opportunity to rebuild. But not just rebuild. Rebuild stronger. Rebuild better. Rebuild smarter. Because if you let your pain define you, it will. If you let your wounds be the last word in your story, that's where the book ends. But I'm not done with you yet. And you shouldn't be either.

It's easy to think that when you've been through hell—whether that's a relationship falling apart, the death of a loved one, addiction, or anything else that shatters your life—that you'll never be whole again. You look at the pieces of yourself, scattered and broken, and wonder if they can ever be put back together. And here's the kicker: **they can.** Not only can they be put back together, but they can come back even stronger than before.

Think about it like this: When something breaks, it's just an opportunity to rebuild it in a way that works for you, in a way that makes sense for the life you're building now. **Every scar, every flaw, every crack in**

your soul is just a testament to the fact that you're still here. And here's the beauty of it—those cracks? They're not weaknesses. They're where the light gets in. They're where the growth happens.

Look, life is full of shit you can't control. We all know that. We all wish we could wave a magic wand and avoid the heartache, the mistakes, the betrayals, the losses. But if you really think about it—if you're honest with yourself—would you trade those experiences for anything? Would you want to go back to a life that's easy, comfortable, and predictable? Hell no. Because you know that the pain, the heartbreak, and the suffering were the very things that pushed you to rise up, to face the fire, and to become something better. **Stronger. Wiser. Unbreakable.**

Here's the truth: You are not defined by what's happened to you. You're defined by how you choose to respond to it. Every time you get knocked down, you have a choice. You can stay there, feel sorry for yourself, and tell yourself the same sad story over and over again. Or, you can look at your scars, own them, and use them as fuel to rebuild. Every damn time. And I don't care how many times you get knocked down. What matters is that you get up, dust yourself off, and rebuild stronger.

I know what it's like to feel like you're beyond repair. Hell, there was a time when I thought I was done. When I thought there was no way out of the hole I was in. I've been broken, lost, addicted, and on the verge of losing everything. But every time I fell, I had to pick myself back up. **And that's when I realized—rebuilding wasn't just about picking up the pieces. It was about changing the way I looked at the whole damn thing.**

It's about shifting your mindset from "I can't do this" to "I'm gonna do this, even if it's hard as hell." It's about taking your pain, your fear, your failures, and saying, "Okay, what now?" What are you going to do with all that shit? Are you going to let it break you? Or are you going to turn it into your foundation?

Here's a little secret: You don't have to do it alone. Rebuilding isn't about being some solitary, superhuman warrior who doesn't need anyone. The most powerful people in the world have a team behind them. They have people who support them, people who lift them up, people who help them see their own value when they can't see it themselves. So yeah, reach out for help. Get the support you need. **But don't ever forget that the true strength lies in you.**

It's your responsibility to rebuild. Nobody's coming to save you. And that's the best damn thing that could ever happen. Because once you realize that no one's going to fix your shit, you'll stop waiting for someone else to do it. You'll get up, you'll take responsibility, and you'll start putting the pieces together, one by one. No more excuses, no more blaming others. **It's on you.**

And when you do rebuild, don't just rebuild what was there before. Build something better. Build something that works for you. Build a life that reflects the lessons you've learned and the strength you've gained. Don't settle for the same shit you had before. **Demand better. Demand more.**

When you rebuild stronger, you rebuild smarter. You make better choices. You stop settling for toxic relationships. You stop drinking away your pain. You stop ignoring the things that truly matter. Rebuilding isn't just about physical or emotional strength—it's about wisdom. It's about learning what works and what doesn't. And more than anything, it's about understanding that the things you thought were your greatest failures, your deepest scars, and your darkest moments are actually the things that make you *unbreakable*.

So go ahead, take your broken self, your shattered pieces, and **build something amazing out of it.** Don't just survive—**thrive.** Rebuild stronger. Rebuild better. Rebuild with intention, with purpose, and with the understanding that you're not just putting yourself back together—you're creating something new, something stronger, something unstoppable.

And when you're done, you'll look at the person you've become and realize that the pain, the heartache, and the struggles were all worth it. Because they made you who you are. And who you are is pretty damn extraordinary.

So rebuild. And never, ever, stop getting stronger.

CHAPTER THIRTY FIVE

Unbreakable as F*ck

Here's the deal: life is gonna throw all sorts of shit at you. People will betray you, the system will screw you, your own mind will try to sabotage you—and yet, you'll still stand. Why? Because you're unbreakable as f*ck.

I'm not talking about being some perfect, infallible version of yourself. Nope. That's not real. Real life isn't about having it all together. Real life is about getting knocked down, being bruised, and still finding the strength to stand up again—over and over and over again. It's about looking at everything life throws at you and saying, "Is that all you've got?"

It's easy to feel like the universe is out to get you. It's easy to feel like you're constantly swimming against a tide of bad luck, poor decisions, and people who want to see you fail. And yeah, some of that shit can break you for a minute. Maybe for longer than a minute. But here's what no one tells you: **you are so much stronger than you realize.** The more they knock you down, the harder you get back up. The more the world throws at you, the more you realize that none of it can keep you down forever. Because you? **You are unbreakable.**

Now, don't get it twisted. Being unbreakable doesn't mean you won't bend, crack, or even fall apart for a second. It's not about being perfect—it's about what you do when the sh*t hits the fan. It's about what you do when you hit rock bottom and you're staring up at the abyss, wondering how the hell you're going to crawl out of it.

I've been there. Oh, I've been there. You know the kind of pain where it feels like the weight of the world is crushing you and all you want to do is crawl into a hole and never come out? Yeah, I've been there. But here's the thing: I didn't stay there. **I refused to stay there.** And you need to refuse to stay there too.

Because, my friend, it's in those moments that your true power emerges. The strength you didn't know you had starts showing up. The resilience that you thought you didn't have a *fcking clue about starts becoming your new best friend.* ***You get up, you dust yourself off, and you keep fcking going.***

And don't you dare think you're doing this alone. I don't care how independent you are, how badass you think you are—there's always someone who's got your back. Maybe it's a friend, maybe it's a mentor, maybe it's just the sheer force of your own will. But **you are never alone in this fight**. You are always connected to something bigger, something that keeps you going when you want to quit.

The real secret? The more you go through, the more you learn to adapt. The more you realize that nothing, and I mean nothing, can actually break you. Oh, they'll try. They'll throw their punches. People will let you down, and you'll think the world's against you. But you know what? Every time it happens, you get a little tougher. Every failure, every heartbreak, every betrayal just adds another layer to that unbreakable foundation.

You are the f*cking storm, not the victim of it. You are the one who walks through the fire and comes out on the other side not just unscathed, but stronger, more resilient, more *unbreakable* than ever.

So here's what I want you to remember: don't ever let anyone or anything convince you that you're broken. Don't let the world tell you that you can't rise from your ashes. You're not a fragile thing that's going to fall apart the moment things get hard. You're a *fcking warrior. You're unbreakable as f*ck.* So stand tall, wear your scars like the badges of honor they are, and keep f*cking going.

Because the world may try to break you, but it will never succeed. **You're unbreakable as f*ck.** And nothing, not a damn thing, is going to change that.

Part Eight: The Legacy of Imperfection

If there's one thing I've learned after all the bullshit, after all the pain, and the struggles that life has thrown at me, it's this: **Perfection is a myth.** It's an illusion, a dream we're fed since we're kids, and we chase it like it's the holy grail. But guess what? Perfection doesn't exist. And if you've been trying to live up to that impossible standard, it's time to stop. You don't need to be perfect to leave a legacy. In fact, it's your imperfections—the scars, the mistakes, the wrong turns—that make your story worth telling.

In this final part, we're talking about leaving behind something that matters. Something that's real. Something that shows the world that you didn't just go through life being another cookie-cutter, perfect little puppet. You lived. You messed up. You rose, you fell, you f*cked up again and again—and somehow, you still managed to come out on the other side stronger, better, and more unapologetically you.

This is the part where we dive into the real reason we're here. Why we do what we do. Why we fight when everything seems stacked against us. Because we're not just here to survive—we're here to **leave a mark.** A real one. One that's made from the messy, complicated, beautifully flawed version of ourselves. We don't need to be flawless to matter. We just need to be real.

The legacy we leave isn't about doing things perfectly. It's about showing up, facing down the chaos, and saying, "I was here. I f*cked up, I learned, and I did the best I could with what I had." And that's more than enough.

So buckle up, because in Part Eight, we're going to get deep into what it means to leave behind a legacy that's real. We're talking about embracing our imperfections and using them as the foundation for a life that's meaningful. No more chasing some bullshit idea of perfection. The real power comes from owning who you are—flaws and all—and building something from that.

By the end of this part, you'll see that it's not about being perfect. It's about being **authentically, unapologetically, and beautifully imperfect**. It's about making sure that when people look at your life, they don't see some polished, fake version of who you were. They see the raw, real, unfiltered you. That's your legacy. And trust me, it's more than enough. It's everything.

CHAPTER THIRTY SIX

What Will You Leave Behind?

It's a tough question, isn't it? One we don't often ask ourselves—what the hell are we actually leaving behind when it's all said and done? Because, let's face it, none of us are getting out of here alive. We can sit around pretending we've got forever, but time is ticking away, whether we like it or not. So, what's the mark you're going to leave on this world? What's going to be your legacy?

Here's the thing: the answer isn't about the stuff you collect, the money you make, or how perfect your life seems on the outside. It's not about the Instagram-worthy photos or the "I've got my shit together" facade we all try to put up. No. It's about something deeper, something real. It's about the **impact** you make. The lives you touch, the people you help, the way you make others feel seen, heard, and understood. It's about the example you set, not of perfection, but of resilience, of growth, of living with your whole heart—even when life is a mess.

The truth is, most of us will never have our names in lights. We won't be remembered for winning awards or making the big bucks. But we don't need to be. The real legacy comes from the way we live our lives, how we deal with failure, how we treat others, and whether or not we choose to keep going when everything tells us to quit. **That's what people will remember.** How you lived through the mess, how you owned your shit, how you weren't afraid to fail and get back up, how you loved fiercely, laughed often, and showed up, even when life tried to knock you out.

You might not get a statue built in your honor, and you might not write a book that everyone remembers. But guess what? You don't have to. Because your legacy isn't about what you do for the world—it's about what you do for the people who matter most. It's about how you've loved, how you've been there for others, how you've shown up in your own life and the lives of those around you.

So, I want you to think long and hard about this: **What will you leave behind?** Will it be the perfect social media feed, the neatly packaged version of your life that everyone expects to see? Or will it be the real, unfiltered version of who you are—the one who f*cks up, gets up, keeps going, loves hard, and lives authentically?

You get to choose. Every single day. And the best part? Your legacy doesn't have to be perfect—it just has to be real. It just has to be **you.**

So, are you ready to leave a legacy that matters? One that speaks of strength, of love, of realness? The kind that isn't afraid to be imperfect and still stand tall, knowing that you've given everything you've got? Because that's the legacy worth leaving behind.

The one that says, "I was here. I lived, I loved, I f*cked up, and I never stopped trying." And that's more than enough. That's everything.

CHAPTER THIRTY SEVEN

F*ck Perfect, Be Real

Here's the brutal truth: **Perfection is a trap.** A shiny, glittery, impossible trap that we're all suckered into at some point. Society sells us this idea that if we just do everything right—look perfect, say the right things, act a certain way, be successful, have it all together—then, and only then, will we be worthy. Worthy of love, worthy of success, worthy of being seen. But you know what? It's all bullshit.

Perfect is a lie. A myth. A fleeting moment in time that's impossible to hold onto. It doesn't exist. And yet, we chase it like it's the holy grail, hoping that when we finally achieve it, we'll feel like we're enough. But let me tell you something—**you don't need to be perfect to be enough.**

In fact, the more you chase perfection, the further away you get from being real. Because when you're obsessed with being flawless, you start to hide the parts of you that make you, *you*. The raw, messy, beautiful, broken parts that are the real magic of your story. The parts of you that aren't perfect, but that are real. That's where the magic happens.

So why the hell are we still pretending? Why are we still letting the world tell us who we should be, how we should look, and how we should live? It's time to say, **f*ck it.** Let's throw perfection out the window and start living like the real, imperfect, messy humans that we are.

You don't need to have it all figured out. You don't need to be the perfect spouse, the perfect friend, the perfect parent, the perfect anything. You just need to be **real.** Raw, unfiltered, unapologetically you. With all your flaws, your scars, your mistakes, your quirks, and your moments of absolute chaos. Because that's where the power is. That's where the beauty is.

I'm not saying we should give up on trying to be better. We should always strive to grow, to learn, to improve. But we need to stop holding ourselves to the impossible standard of perfection. We need to stop pretending like we have all the answers. We need to stop worrying about what people think and just start being who we really are—flaws and all.

Imagine what would happen if we all stopped pretending to be perfect. Imagine if we could just be real with each other—vulnerable, raw, messy. Do you know how much freedom that would bring? How much strength it would take to stand up and say, "This is who I am. Take it or leave it. But this is me—imperfect, broken, beautiful, and f*cking real."

The truth is, **the world doesn't need another perfect person.** It needs real ones. It needs people who aren't afraid to show up as themselves, no matter how flawed they might seem. It needs you. The real you. Not the version you think you should be to fit in. Not the one you put on when you want to impress others. The one who is bold, messy, and free. The one who says, "I'm not perfect, and that's okay."

So, I'm here to tell you—**f*ck perfect.** It's overrated, it's exhausting, and it's just one big lie. Be real. Be honest. Be raw. Be messy. And most importantly, be **you.** The world needs your authenticity more than it needs your perfection. And the best part? You get to stop pretending. You get to show up as yourself—flaws and all—and know that's more than enough.

Perfection can go f*ck itself. It's time to be real.

Conclusion: The F*ck Perfect Manifesto

So, here we are, at the end of this wild ride. Or maybe it's the middle, or the beginning of something new. Honestly, who the hell knows? Life doesn't have clear-cut endings or beginnings; it just is. One chaotic, unpredictable, beautiful mess. And that's exactly what this book is about. But don't get it twisted—this isn't the end. It's just another step in the journey. Whether it's the end of this book or the beginning of something bigger, you and I both know that the story isn't over. We've just reached a new chapter, and where it goes from here is up to you—and me.

And I'll tell you this: the one thing I've learned about life, art, and everything in between is that nothing is set in stone. Not the music, not the books, not your path, and definitely not the f*cked-up shit that we get caught up in. I may have written three books already, and yes, this one is the "final" one. But you know what? I can't promise you that there won't be more. You think I'm done? You think I've spilled every ounce of blood, sweat, and soul into these pages? Maybe. Maybe not.

You see, art doesn't come with deadlines, and neither does life. Every time I think I'm done, I find another piece of myself to explore. Another layer to peel back. Another f*cked-up story to tell. Hell, if you think about it, this whole book was supposed to be a "bonus," something I wasn't even planning to write. But here we are. So don't sit there thinking I'm going to walk away from my music or my words just because I wrote the last page. The truth is, **I don't know** what's next. And that's exactly the point.

If I've learned anything from my own life, it's that nothing is ever really finished. Life is messy, unpredictable, and infinitely complex. So when people ask, "What's next for you, Derrick?" or "Are you done with books and music?" I always have the same answer: **Who the f*ck knows?** I'm just here, doing my thing, and I can't tell you what the future holds. But I can promise you one thing: if I've got something to say, I'll say it. Whether it's through a song, a book, or just a conversation over a beer, I'll keep speaking my truth—because that's the only thing I really know how to do.

That brings me to this, the heart of everything I've shared in these pages: the **F*ck Perfect Manifesto**. It's not just some snarky title. It's a declaration of everything I stand for. Everything that matters, and everything I've learned. It's about living life on **your** terms. Being **you**, no matter how messy, imperfect, or f*cked up you think you are. It's about dropping the mask, rejecting the bullshit, and just **being real** with yourself and the world around you.

But here's the thing: the **manifesto** isn't just for me. It's for **you** too. And it's for anyone who's ever been told they're not enough. Anyone who's felt pressure to conform, to fit in, to be the version of themselves that society says they should be. It's for the rebels, the outcasts, the ones who aren't afraid to screw up and get back up again. The ones who know that life isn't about getting it right every time. It's about showing up and being real, even when you don't have all the answers. Especially when you don't have all the answers.

This is your manifesto too. A manifesto for people who understand that **perfection is a lie.** That it's okay to fail, it's okay to fall, and it's okay to feel like absolute shit sometimes. But the key is **to keep going**—to rise, to dust yourself off, and to keep moving forward, even when it feels like the world is trying to drag you down. You're not perfect, and that's exactly why you're beautiful.

So, do I know what's coming next in my journey? Maybe I'll write another book. Maybe I'll drop a new album. Hell, maybe I'll just take a break and live my life. The point is, **it doesn't matter.** What matters is that whatever I do, whatever I create, and wherever this journey takes me—I'm going to keep it real. I'm going to keep sharing my story, my pain, my joy, my growth, and every damn thing in between. Because that's all I've got to give. That's my truth. And if you've learned anything from this book, it's that **your truth** is the most powerful weapon you have.

To everyone who's been on this ride with me—thank you. You've made this possible. You've made my story your own. And if you take one thing from this book, let it be this: **Don't you dare try to be perfect.** Live for the messy, the real, and the unapologetically f*cked-up moments that make life worth living. If you can do that, then you're doing it right.

Maybe this is the end. Maybe it's not. Either way, this is where I stand. Real. Raw. Imperfect. And proud as f*ck.

So here's the manifesto, in all its glory:

- F*ck perfect.
- Be real.
- Show up, no matter how messy.
- Fail forward.
- Love hard, even when it's scary.
- Laugh at your f*ck-ups.
- Don't take shit from anyone.
- Keep your boundaries tight and your heart open.
- Own your ugly.
- Leave the world a little bit better than you found it.

And remember, no matter where life takes us: **You are enough. Just as you are.** Always.

Derrick Solano is a survivor, storyteller, and unapologetic advocate for living authentically. From a tumultuous childhood in the foster care system to battles with addiction, heartbreak, and loss, Derrick has faced life's hardest challenges head-on, turning his scars into fuel for resilience and growth. His memoir, **I Won't Break**, became a rallying cry for those fighting to rise after life knocks them down. In his follow-up books, *Vexture* and *NAKED*, Derrick explored the power of owning pain, redefining success, and stripping away societal expectations to live fully and freely.

Now with his bonus book, **F*ck Perfect**, Derrick brings his no-holds-barred honesty and raw humor to complete his story, offering readers the ultimate guide to breaking free from the myth of perfection and living unapologetically real. A fierce believer in the strength of vulnerability, Derrick continues to inspire others through his writing, music, and podcast. When not creating, he shares a peaceful life in Las Vegas, New Mexico, with his husband, Anthony, and their pack of rescue dogs.